MENTORING

with

Common Sense

Dr. Roy W. Harris

Brother Dwayne,

I hope you enjoy the book.

God Bless

Roy W. Harris

4/24/15

To order additional copies of this book contact

Dr. Roy W. Harris
906 Castle Heights Ave.
Lebanon, Tennessee 37087
roy@royharris.info
615-351-1425

Order Online
@
www.royharris.info

FWB

About the Author

Dr. Roy W. Harris pours decades of mentoring experience into the pages of *MENTORING with Common Sense.*

He mentored hundreds of students during his 16-year tenure as a staff, faculty and administration member of Welch College in Nashville, TN.

Dr. Harris is an ordained minister and veteran pastor having pastored churches in North Carolina, Georgia, Tennessee and Kentucky. He oversaw and mentored staffs of one to twenty-four employees.

He continues mentoring both young and old across America and across the ocean in Kenya, Tanzania, and Uganda.

Dr. Harris holds Bachelor of Arts and Master of Ministry degrees from Welch College and a Doctor of Philosophy degree in Pastoral Ministry from Trinity Theological Seminary.

Table of Contents

RECOMMENDED *by men* Roy **MENTORED**...

"In *MENTORING with Common Sense,* Dr. Roy Harris writes about a subject he knows well. I've experienced Dr. Harris' mentoring skills firsthand as a student at Welch College. This book is especially needed today. If churches and families are to be successful, they need to engage in the mentoring principles described in this book. You'll enjoy reading the book and I highly recommend it."

Dr. Eddie Moody, *Chair of the Department of Counselor Education, North Carolina Central University and Pastor of Tippet's Chapel Church.*

"There is a vast difference between writing about mentoring and actually doing it. Dr. Roy Harris is well qualified to write on the subject. He has successfully mentored countless young men through decades of ministry. I am one of his mentees. He has been my mentor for over 28 years. Dr. Harris has developed proven principles that work in the context of life and ministry. All who aspire to lead others will do well to read and keep *MENTORING with Common Sense* close at hand."

Reverend Tim Campbell, *Executive Director, Arkansas State Association of Free Will Baptists.*

"To read a book is one thing, but to know the author is quite another. Dr. Roy Harris was my mentor during a crucial time in my spiritual and professional development. I personally experienced Dr. Harris' *common sense* approach to mentoring and it made a significant difference in my life."

Reverend Stewart-Allen Clark, *Lead Pastor, First General Baptist Church, Malden, MO.*

Introduction

A simple definition of the word mentor is *trusted advisor, counselor,* and *teacher* according to the Oxford Dictionary. Many etymologists trace the origin to Mentor, a character in Homer's *Odyssey*, who was a trusted friend of Odysseus.

The word *mentor,* in the modern era, first surfaced in the mid-seventeen hundreds. It has experienced a huge resurgence in the past ten years or so and now is a red-hot term used in a variety of venues.

Mentoring is nothing new. Mentors, mentoring and people receiving mentoring have taken place since men first began to walk the earth.

The character of mentors, the receptiveness of those who are candidates for mentoring, and the approach taken by mentors all play a huge role in the success or failure of the mentoring process.

Most people are the sum total of the investment (mentoring) that others poured into their lives. We are who we are because of what others saw in us and thought we could become.

We have a responsibility to *pay it forward* by investing in the lives of others and helping them become the people God intends for them to be.

This author penned *MENTORING with Common Sense* to guide others in developing the skills necessary to become successful mentors.

The book takes prospective mentors on an easy to understand step-by-step journey down the mentoring road.

Mentoring requires investing time, talent, and treasure, but the rewards are well worth the investment. Often mentors receive as much, if not more from mentoring others as those who receive the mentoring.

Read this book with an attitude of prayer, a desire to invest in the lives of others, and a willingness to learn. You may be amazed at what God may do with and through you and the tremendous impact you will make in the lives of others.

CHAPTER 1

Who Mentored You?

I secured my first job at age 13 delivering newspapers to homes in our neighborhood, learning the basics about earning money and responsibility. Anderson, Indiana, was a great mid-western town and a great place to grow up.

At 16 my career at a fast food restaurant called Burger Chef began with cleaning restrooms, emptying trashcans, mopping floors, etc. I quickly rose up the employee ladder. I moved to the back line preparing sandwiches and French fries. I was promoted to the front line taking and filling orders for customers.

At age 17 I was promoted to assistant manager and then night manager. My responsibilities included but were not limited to overseeing up to eight employees at a time, handling thousands of dollars in daily sales and preparing nightly bank deposits. I was well on my way down the road to success as a young man.

I saved my money, purchased my own car, bought my own clothes and was doing well for my age.

One day I received a phone call from my pastor, Reverend Ed Hargis. I had never received a call from my pastor before, so I was a little uneasy and nervous when my mother handed me the phone. The voice on the other end was direct and to the point.

My pastor asked if I would meet him at the church a little early before the evening service? He said he had something he needed to talk with me about. I agreed to meet him but was uneasy wondering what he wanted to talk with me about.

When I arrived at church, he was waiting in his office. You will never guess what he wanted to talk with me about and what he said to me...

At the end of this chapter, I'll tell you what he said and what happened in his office that day and how it impacted my life then and continues to impact my life today.

If asked who influenced your life and helped you become the person you are today, who would come to your mind almost immediately? George Eliot once said: "Blessed is the influence of one true, loving human soul on another."

Oprah Winfrey was impacted greatly by her fourth grade teacher, Mrs. Mary Duncan. Winfrey credits Mrs. Duncan with having one of the greatest influences on her life. I'm not an Oprah Winfrey fan but she makes a statement about mentors and mentoring that is worth repeating:

> "A mentor is someone who allows you to see the hope inside yourself. A mentor is someone who allows you to know that no matter how dark the night; in the morning joy will come. A mentor is someone who allows you to see the higher part of yourself when sometimes it becomes hidden to your own view. I don't think anybody makes it in the world without some form of mentorship. And we are all mentors to people, even when we don't know it."

We are who we are because of the influence and impact of others on our lives. We may not consciously recognize the ways we've been influenced. What and why we do things in life many times grow from the roots of those who influenced us by the way they did it.

We each have a responsibility to influence and impact the lives of others. We owe a debt for what we received from others and can only repay that debt by investing in the lives of still yet others.

We may not think of them every day, and years may have passed since they crossed our minds. But we all have people who've impacted our lives.

They saw something special in us and invested their time, experiences, and wisdom. They were willing to pour into our lives the overflow from theirs. They were and are our mentors.

This book could be entirely devoted to those who were my mentors and continue to influence and impact my life. A book devoted to those people would be meaningful and a joy to write, but you wouldn't know most of them and the value would be less to you.

I will mention a number of those people and also others throughout the book who are examples of mentors worthy of imitating. I'll draw principles, suggestions, and lessons from their examples and my own personal experience as a mentor to reproduce personal and spiritual disciplines of Christian maturity in future mentors.

Now back to my pastor and me in his office. My pastor's son, Keith Hargis, and I were best friends. He had his life planned for the future. After his senior year of high school, he would attend Welch College (formally Free Will Baptist Bible College) in Nashville, TN, and probably follow in his father's footsteps as a minister.

Keith and I were dating girls who lived in Wabash, IN, a city about an hour north of where we lived in Anderson. My father would not let me work on Sundays.

He believed that working on Sunday was a violation of God's commandment of keeping the Lord's Day holy. He observed it personally and insisted that my brother and I reverence it also.

My boss at Burger Chef called me with an emergency one Sunday morning and begged me to work just for a few hours.

I do not recall what the emergency was, but for some reason my father agreed but said this would be the one and only time he would permit it. I planned to ride with Keith to Wabash and attend church with our girlfriends that Sunday morning.

I worked most of the day shift when dad came by and told me there was an emergency and I needed to come home immediately.

My day boss called another employee scheduled for the evening shift who was able to relieve me. I went home expecting to hear news of a family member passing away only to find out it was something much different.

My dad shared with me that my close friend Keith had been killed in an automobile accident on his way to Wabash. Evidently, a car pulled out in front of him.

He swerved to miss the car and his car rolled over throwing him from the car and into the path of his rolling vehicle. He was crushed and died under his own vehicle. My good friend was dead!

I'm in the office with my pastor, the father of my good friend who had died only months ago. What did he say and do that day that impacted my life then and still continues to impact me today?

He said this to me: "Roy, are you planning to flip hamburgers the rest of your life? I believe God has something very special for you to do. I see something in you that I believe God can and wants to use. I want you to pray and consider going to Free Will Baptist Bible College this fall."

He made me angry that evening. I thought he didn't appreciate how hard I'd worked to get where I was at Burger Chef. He didn't realize I had my life planned and Bible College was the furthest thing from it.

But something began to happen to me after I left his office that evening. I began thinking about what he'd said. He saw something in me that he thought was special.

He believed God had something special in life for me to do. The more I thought about what he said the more God dealt with my heart.

I struggled with the nagging thought that my plans were not God's plans for my life. I tried to get away from what my pastor had said to me the rest of my senior year and most of the summer after I graduated from high school.

By the end of the summer I was convinced that if I did not at least enroll and attend Welch College for one year that God would make life very difficult for me.

I was able, through my mother's extraordinary efforts, to enroll at Welch College one week before the school year began. I surrendered my life to God's service during the campus revival and heard the quiet voice of God's Holy Spirit reveal to me a few weeks later what He had revealed to my pastor many months before.

God's special plan for me was to become one of His ambassadors heralding the Good News of the Gospel as His messenger. God called me to be one of His preachers.

Why relate this story to you? You see, my pastor prayed for me and God impressed him to press me about my future.

Brother Hargis told me later that God had spoken to his heart and informed him that He had something special for me to do in life. I'm so glad my pastor listen to the Lord and cared enough to confront me.

I never got away from what he told me that evening in his office. I remember it like it was yesterday. It has been a source of strength and encouragement to me through the years and still today.

I'm reminded that my mentor saw something special in me, and he cared enough to tell me that God's plan is always the best plan.

We should be sensitive to God's leadership in our lives, as He impresses us to press others about their present and future. I believe one of the gifts the Holy Spirit imparts to mentors is the gift of discernment.

We should be on the lookout for those special people for whom God has special plans.

Someone tapped us on the shoulder and now it's our turn to tap others. Second Timothy 2:2 reminds us that we have a responsibility to pass along to others what we've heard from faithful men and women, so they can continue the process and pass it along to others also.

God's will for Keith was to take him on to be with Him in heaven. His plan for me was what I thought was his plan for Keith, to be a minister proclaiming the good news of Jesus Christ to a world that desperately needs it. Guess what? God's plan is the best plan.

My life has been rich with His blessings and full with opportunities of service. I could never have dreamed what God had in store for me sitting in my pastor's office at age 17.

I'm so thankful for a godly pastor who loved me, prayed for me, and confronted me to become all I could be for the Lord.

Brother Hargis joined his son several years ago. I had the privilege of being a pallbearer along with some other men he'd impacted.

I carried this godly man to his place of rest who'd carried me to my place of service.

I'm sure the Lord greeted Brother Hargis at Heaven's gate with, "Well done thou good and faithful servant." One day I'll be able to join him and my good friend Keith and thank him again for being my example, my friend, and my MENTOR.

CHAPTER 2

The Moses Model

There is no better place than the Word of God to look for examples of mentoring. God's use of mentoring in selecting, equipping, and sending out His servants to disseminate the Good News of the gospel, leaps off the pages of God's Word.

Jonathon mentored David, Elijah mentored Elisha, Paul mentored Timothy, and the *Supreme Mentor,* Jesus, mentored the original twelve Disciples.

The Moses Mentoring Model

One early example of mentoring in the Bible is found in the book of Exodus with one of God's choice servant, Moses.

Moses was mentored by an unknown and unnamed someone(s) in Pharaoh's court in the practices, protocol, politics, and procedures of the Egyptian culture and government. He moved with ease within the inner circles of power and government for 40 years.

The Bible is silent on how he became polished in Egyptian culture. No doubt his Egyptian stepmother impacted him greatly.

But the wisdom and knowledge he gained served him well when he returned at age 80 to the court to plead

for the release of God's people after a 40-year absence.

God used others in preparing him to confront the most powerful kingdom on earth in his generation.

A desert herdsman named Jethro, who become Moses father-in-law, mentored Moses in a totally different culture. Moses learned much under Jethro's wise instruction for 40 more years.

What a contrast. He moved from a palace of royalty to the tent of a shepherd. He laid down the crook and flail, symbols of Egyptian power and authority, and picked up the staff, the tool of shepherds.

God used tutors of royalty and a simple man from the desert in mentoring Moses who became one of the greatest leaders the world has known.   What did he learn?

Obviously it is impossible to adequately answer that question, but there is one thing we know for sure. He understood the value of pouring one's life into the lives of others.

The palace and the pasture molded the first 80 years of Moses' life preparing him to fulfill God's purpose during the last 40 years of his life.

Part of God's purpose was to lead the children of Israel from Egyptian bondage and prepare them to enter the land that had been promised.

Another part of God's purpose for Moses was to mentor a successor who would lead in conquering and occupying the Promised Land. Joshua was selected and learned under the mentorship of Moses for 40 years.

Bill Hull on page 56 his book *The Complete Book of Discipleship: Being & Making followers of Christ*, (Navpress, 2006) does a great job discussing the mentoring relationship between Jethro, Aaron, Moses and Joshua.

His description of their relationships is manifested into five characteristics does a good job of describing what I've named the Moses Mentoring Model.

I'll summarize these and recast them a bit.

Let me share with you five principles of The Moses Mentoring Model.

1. *Nurture the Relationship*. Moses was impacted by a number of men. Jethro his father-in-law and Aaron his brother were key influences that encouraged and helped him along the way. They did this through years of gaining each other's confidence with ongoing growing relationships.

Moses learned from these and other relationships and began the mentoring process with Joshua by building a close and growing relationship with him. Moses inaugurated his mentorship with Joshua when he took him up on the mountain with him to meet God.

The relationship continued with Joshua becoming an almost constant companion to the great leader. Where you saw Moses, Joshua was nearby.

2. *Competence is gained through Apprenticeship*. Joshua was an apprentice leader under Moses' mentorship and probably didn't know God would assign him his mentor's role one day. He served as an apprentice for many years under Moses the skilled leader.

Joshua observed his mentor in a variety of circumstances and situations. He saw Moses in the good times and bad times.

He watched Moses accomplish great things and also make mistakes. Joshua observed Moses' behavior and reactions in all kinds of situations and no doubt learned a great deal from many of them.

There is great value in working close to someone and observing them in a variety of situations. I personally like the word *apprentice* better than *intern*.

Apprentices study under master craftsmen who pass along skills to others who will one day take their places. Apprentices are by the side of master craftsmen learning by watching through project after project.

3. *Confidence is gained through Accountability*. Moses learned a great deal during his apprenticeship days while being mentored by his father-in-law Jethro. He learned from Jethro the importance of delegating responsibility and holding people accountable for the accomplishment of the tasks assigned to them.

No doubt Jethro delegated many tasks to Moses during their 40 years together prior to Moses return to Egypt.

Joshua observed Moses' management style and was assigned specific tasks to which he would be accountable. By being held accountable and successfully completing what was expected of him, he gained confidence in his own ability to delegate, evaluate, reward, or chastise.

Joshua learned a great deal about accountability and confidence by observing Moses' management style.

4. *Successful mentoring requires submission in the short term and loyalty for the long haul from those who are mentored*. Joshua recognized that he had much to learn. He didn't have all the answers and didn't know all the questions yet. He willingly submitted himself to Moses.

Joshua understood that molding and shaping comes from the hands of a skilled craftsman. Moses was a master craftsman, and Joshua placed himself in submission into the hands of the skilled master craftsman leader.

Forty years is a long time to stand in the shadow of someone else. It took forty years for the complaining, dissatisfied, unbelieving crowd to pass from the scene.

Joshua and Caleb were the only ones from their generation to enter the Promised Land. God let Moses see it from a distance but even Moses didn't make it in alive.

More will be mentioned about *loyalty* later but I want to mention it briefly here. Joshua remained loyal to Moses for the long hall. For forty years he faithful followed the instructions and assignments of his mentor. For forty years he fulfilled his responsibilities knowing that he was accountable to Moses.

Joshua saw Moses' strengths and stamina but also his faults and frailty. He knew Moses was not perfect, and Joshua learned that he did not have to be either.

Other seemingly import people opposed Moses at times and I'm sure invited Joshua to join them with promises of position, prestige and prominence.

Joshua rejected their overtures, content to be number two instead of the top man. He remained loyal to his mentor until his mentor was no longer on the scene.

I'm sure as Joshua faced multiple leadership challenges he automatically dropped his mental bucket deep into the well of those mentored lessons he'd learned while under submission and instruction of his mentor Moses.

Submission and Loyalty, two key ingredients Moses successfully passed on to Joshua.

5. *The Mentored becomes the Mentor.* Joshua waited a long time and remained content and faithfully served where God placed him. But the time came when Moses stepped down as leader.

Joshua was ready. He was ready to become the leader of Israel. He was competent, confident, and compelled by God as he stepped into a role that he may not have imagined.

Now it was his turn to be the mentor for future leaders of Israel. The mentored became the mentor.

The endgame of the Moses Mentoring Model is the endless cycle of passing on to faithful men and women things we've learn so they will be able to teach others also.

2 Timothy 2:2 - *And the things that thou hast heard of me among many witnesses, the same commit thou to faithful men, who shall be able to teach others also.*

CHAPTER 3

Who Makes Good Mentors?

The school board in my hometown of Anderson, Indiana, had an unusual approach to learning. I must say I agree with one unique idea they had for us in junior high school.

They required seventh grade boys right alongside the girls to take *home economics,* learning how to sew and cook in order to survive as bachelors later on in life.

They also required eighth grade girls, right beside the boys, to take *general shop,* learning the basics of changing a tire, using jumper cables to start a car, checking oil and transmission fluids, etc.

Our *home economics* class was divided into two groups. While one group worked on projects in the sewing area, I made a reversible vest – I can tell you're impressed, the other group learned to prepare food in the kitchen area.

One day my group was in the kitchen area. I was given the assignment of preparing oatmeal cookies. Recipes were stored in a small card box. An old-fashioned cartridge pen had been used to write down the list of ingredients and instructions for each recipe.

My teacher handed me the handwritten recipe for oatmeal cookies on a 3 x 5 index card. I began to gather and mix the ingredients. Someone had spilled water on part of the card and the ink had run.

I was doing fine until I came to the amount of one ingredient that I couldn't quite make out. It said ½ _____. It sure looked like ½ cup to me, so I put in a ½ cup of_____.

At the end of this chapter I'll finish the story and tell you what the ½ cup ingredient was and how the cookies turned out.

You might ask *what do oatmeal cookies have to do with good mentors?* Not all oatmeal cookies turn out well or taste good. The same can be said of mentors. Not everyone makes a good mentor.

Just like using the correct ingredients make good cookies, possessing the right characteristics is necessary to be a good mentor. What are some of those characteristics?

Characteristics of Good Mentors

- *Good mentors know the Divine Mentor well.*

Mentoring is done every day by a variety of people. Granted, mentoring is not limited to the Christian world and can be done without the spiritual dynamic in the outside world. Many basic principles of mentoring can be applied without the spiritual dynamic in place.

But in *Kingdom work,* the whole matter may become a house of cards, eventually doomed to possible collapse and failure without the help and direction of God's *Holy Spirit.* Good mentors must be spiritual people. They must know the Lord and know Him well.

Those who want to mentor others should be further down the road of life's experiences than those they hope to mentor. They must be more mature in their walk with Christ, their faith, and their personal maturity than those they will be mentoring.

- *Good mentors are still learning from the Divine Mentor.*

Those who effectively mentor others continually strive to grow. They want to stretch themselves. They want to hear from the Divine Mentor.

They want to learn more and more from Him about Him. They understand that they have not arrived spiritually.

Even though they've learned a great deal about living and life, they know there is much more yet to learn. They are willing to make the effort and invest the time in hearing and learning from the Divine Mentor Jesus Christ.

- *Good mentors recognize their capabilities and limitations.*

Good mentors know what they can and cannot do. They know their strengths and how to use them to instruct and guide those they mentor. They believe that God created their mentees unique and special.

They understand that mentoring is not about producing exact replicas of them, but helping mentees grow into the person, leader, teacher, etc. that God wants them to be. Good mentors do not create a stereotype mold in their minds and attempt to press mentees into conforming to that mold.

Mentors must also know their weaknesses. Knowing their weaknesses is as important as knowing their strengths.

Wise mentors understand they cannot and do not know everything. They've learned that it is okay to say; *I don't know* when they don't know. Pride and arrogance have no place in the mentoring role. More will be said about this later in the book.

- *Integrity is a must for Mentors.*

This should be understood without saying it, but I will say it anyway. People who say as the apostle Paul did, *follow my model or example* must be people worthy of being followed.

Honesty, purity, morality, etc., should describe Christian mentors. Mentors must live the way they talk. They should never instruct others to behave and live in a manner their own lives do not measure up to.

- *Good Mentors are trustworthy.*

Confidentiality is important in a mentoring relationship. Mentors must know how to keep confidences.

Mentees must believe their mentor can be trusted not to divulge what they've shared in private to anyone else. They must know the mentor will keep private what is shared in private.

- *Good Mentors must possess basic relational skills.*

Good mentors must be able to relate well with individuals one on one. Good people skills are essential to relating well with others.

Comfortably interacting with people enables mentors to build relationships. Mentees will naturally be drawn to people they are comfortable with and whom they feel are comfortable with them.

One way this is accomplished is by communicating effectively with mentees. Communicating effectively with mentees involves more than just conversation.

Mentors must identify where mentees are in their personal and spiritual walks and an honestly evaluate what their potential might be. Mentees must feel their mentors understand them and what is happening in their lives.

- *Good Mentors are open and transparent.*

One of the most effective training tools is personal experience. Personal experience trumps theory every time.

Relating specific personal experiences creates vulnerability for the mentor. Mentors, who are willing to become vulnerable, communicate to mentees that it's okay for them to share personal feelings and experiences.

By becoming vulnerable, mentors help mentees open the door to transparency in their lives.

Mentees are inspired by mentors' successes and encouraged by mentors' failures. Mentors should share past successes. They should also share some of their failures along with times they've been disappointed and hurt in the past. They should talk about their hopes and dreams for the future.

Mentees who hear of mentors' success, failures, hurts, and disappointments find it easier to share their hopes, dreams, failures, hurts, and disappointments.

- *Good Mentors must possess a Giving Spirit.*

I've heard it said on more than one occasion that there are two kinds of people in the world, givers and takers. I'm not sure I necessarily agree with that, but one thing I know from experience. Mentors are givers.

30

Mentoring is work, hard work. It requires commitment. Mentors pour their lives into others. It takes a great deal of time and energy. Good mentors possess and exhibit a giving spirit.

Mentors are willing to commit a portion of their time to *come alongside* their mentees. They willingly exert the emotional and physical energy necessary to guide, lead, push, and pull their mentees across the finish line of progress, accomplishment, and success.

- *Humility characterizes Good Mentors.*

Humility is one of those characteristics that other people see in mentors, and mentors do not easily attribute to themselves. The old expression that when a humble person knows he's humble he is no longer humble.

Humility is the guardrail that helps keep mentors on track. Humility is the quality that reminds mentors where they came from and they still have some distance to go before arriving at perfection. It provides the ability to understand and feel what mentees experience and feel.

Humility is the quality that humanizes mentors in the eyes of mentees. It keeps mentors from ascending the pedestal of pride and shakes them off it if they arrive there and begin to look down from an elevated perch on mentees.

Humility helps mentees understand that mentors are not perfect and are still learning and growing spiritually.

- *Good Mentors are Reliable.*

This is a characteristic that all mentors must possess. Consistency is a must and not optional. Successful mentors live what they teach their mentees.

They must show that what they are asking their mentees to do really can be done and that it produces the desired results.

Mentees are challenged to put the theories they are learning into practice. The mentor must consistently integrate theory with practice and show the theory being practiced.

Mentors build relationships in ways that provide grounds for mentees' belief that they can count on their mentors. More will be said about this later in the book.

- *Discernment is another great characteristic Good Mentors possess.*

Some call it a gut feeling. Some call it a sixth sense.

Whatever one chooses to call it is not important. The important thing is successful mentors seem to always possess it.

What is discernment? Discernment, according to most dictionaries, is *keenly selective judgment*. Good mentors seem to have the ability to size up people and situations quickly and accurately. This is important in the mentoring process.

Good mentors seem to have a knack for sorting out what they hear from mentees.

They can sense when they may need to go deeper into discussions because of what they are hearing. They just seem to know when to press harder or back off in confronting a need or issue.

Let's finish the story about the oatmeal cookies.

Just a reminder - One day my group was in the kitchen area. I was given the assignment of preparing oatmeal cookies.

Recipes were stored in a small card box. An old-fashioned cartridge pen was used to write down the list of ingredients and instructions.

My teacher handed me the handwritten recipe on a 3 x 5 index card. I began to gather and mix the ingredients. Someone had spilled water on part of the card and the ink had run.

I was doing fine until I came to the amount of one ingredient that I couldn't quite make out.

I added a tablespoon of this and a cup of that. The recipe called for soda to be added to the cookie mix. It looked like the recipe called for *½ cup of soda* so I added a *½ cup of soda* and mixed it with the other ingredients.

I placed the cookies in the oven at the proper temperature and for the correct time. They browned nicely, smelled good and looked delicious. When I tasted the cookies they were horrible! They tasted bland like chalk dust, not that I've tasted chalk dust before.

What was wrong with the cookies? The recipe called for *½ teaspoon of baking soda* instead of *½ cup*. Because my ingredients were wrong the cookies turned out wrong and were uneatable.

Not everyone makes a good mentor. They must possess the characteristics necessary to be effective in helping individuals travel down the road of change from where they are to where they need to be.

Aspiring to the role of mentor is a noble ambition. Helping others help themselves is a rewarding endeavor.

But would be mentors should do self-checks to make sure they are competent, compassionate, and committed to what is necessary to insure successful mentoring relationships.

Delicious oatmeal cookies taste good but last only a short period of time. The rewards of mentoring are great!

They can be life changing for mentees and mentors. Unlike cookies, these rewards may last a lifetime.

CHAPTER 4

Benefits for the Mentored

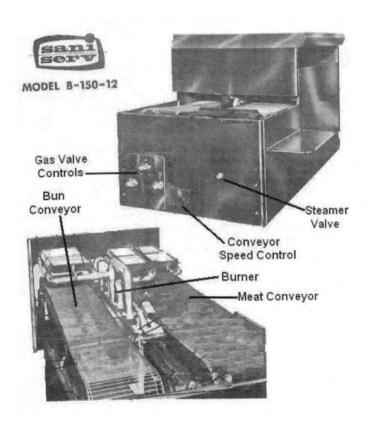

MODEL B-150-12

Gas Valve Controls

Bun Conveyor

Steamer Valve

Conveyor Speed Control

Burner

Meat Conveyor

I arrived home for the summer after completing my freshman year in college, and needed to earn enough money to cover my upcoming college fall semester expenses. I'd been praying about my financial needs and asking the Lord to help me find a good paying job for the summer.

I stopped by Burger Chef to see my old boss Big John and other employee friends. Big John asked if I would come back to his office for a few minutes.

He asked if I would be interested in my old job of managing the night shift. His night manager had moved to another city, and he needed a manager.

I explained that I would be home for the summer and be returning to college in August for the fall semester. He was fine with that, we agreed on a salary package, and I began working the next day.

A few days later, Big John had a surprise for me. He'd been putting off his vacation because he didn't feel he could leave the store. Since he had an experienced manager he could count on (his words), he was going to take a week off and take his wife on vacation.

He wanted me to manage the whole store in his absence. At 18 years of age, I was honored that he had confidence that I could do the job, and a little frightened that maybe I might mess it up somehow.

Then he dropped the big bombshell on me. He said *Roy; while I'm away I want you to also…….*

I'll finish my story at the end of this chapter and tell you what he wanted me to do and how it seemed almost impossible to me at the time.

Benefits for the Mentored

There are great benefits available for individuals who receive good, sound, and competent mentoring from qualified mentors. David J Turner, in his October 28, 2011, online article, does a great job identifying 10 benefits for having a spiritual mentor.

Just as the Bible provides several successful accounts of mentoring, it also describes many benefits mentees may receive through the mentoring process.

There's a grinding wheel located in my shop out back. The grinding wheel is used to sharpen metal objects and remove rough edges.

The action of the spinning wheel traveling at a high rate of speed knocks away rust and impurities from the edge of the metal. The edge is left clean, sharp, shiny, and ready for the tool to be used for the tasks for which it was designed.

Mentors are grinding wheels that God uses to help clean, sharpen, and prepare mentees to successfully attempt and complete the role for which they were created.

Proverbs 27:17 describe friends (mentors) like objects used to sharpen things that need sharpening. The end result of the sharpening process is great improvement (countenance) to the item (mentees), which is sharpened.

Proverbs 4:9-10 gives a very good principle. These verses remind us that two people working together are better than one person alone.

If a person stumbles and falls alone, he has no one to help him up. But the benefits of two people working together are tremendous for both. One will be there to help the other. Two working together stand a better chance of being successful.

Every Christian needs a spiritual mentor. The mentor and the mentee both benefit from the mentoring process.

Granted, for benefits to be received, there must be desire, effort, and reaching out by those who would like to be mentored in order to receive those wonderful mentoring benefits available.

There are at least 10 personal – biblical benefits for those who receive mentoring that provide a lifeline to those being tossed to and fro by the storms of life.

1. *Someone believes in you*.

Everyone needs affirmation. Mentees need someone to believe in them in spite of their imperfections, clutter, and shortcomings. They need someone to be interested in their passions, dreams, and goals for the future.

They need someone they can trust who will listen caringly and provide compassionate, constructive, and objective input while carefully taking into account their sense of how God is working in the mentee's life.

Barnabas' mentoring relationship with John Mark is a great example of this found in Acts 15:36-39, 2 Timothy 4:11.

2. *Mentoring provides a role model or example to follow.*

The apostle Paul is one of the greatest mentors in the New Testament. What was his greatest asset? Obviously the Holy Spirit is always the greatest asset.

Paul gives us a clue to his success as a mentor in 1 Corinthians 11:1 by stating one of the most important principles in mentoring. In summary Paul says, "Follow my example." He's conveying the idea that he is a role model that can be trusted to imitate.

How can he make a statement that strong? The answer is found in the second part of the verse. Paul says that his mentees can safely imitate him as their role model because he is being mentored also.

His role model is the Lord Jesus Christ. Paul says; "imitate me, the way I act, the things that I do and the way I live because I am imitating my great mentor Jesus Christ."

Obviously mentors have a tall order to fill in exampling for mentees the principles they should live by. They can safely do this by continually receiving instructions from their great mentor the Lord Himself and trying to be more like Him every day. Observing a godly life in action is a tremendous benefit to mentees.

3. *Assistance in growing spiritually.*

Mentees receive the great benefit of guidance in developing solid patterns of spiritual discipline in their lives. This will help them deepen their relationship with Christ, grow more like Christ, and be elevated to a higher level of usefulness in His kingdom.

Spiritual life patterns, established early in the mentoring relationship, have the potential of benefiting those mentored for the rest of their lives.

Paul emphasizes in Philippians 3:13 the importance of striving and continually moving forward having matured through the years, knowing the ultimate goal of spiritual maturity.

Mentors promote spiritual growth and establishment of spiritual life patterns by helping mentees with formal and informal Bible study, targeted reading assignments, training in the Christian disciplines, determining spiritual gifts and directions for ministry opportunities. Christian disciplines will be discussed in detail in later chapters.

4. *Someone to be accountable to.*

Today's cultural landscape is filled with immorality magnets, pornographic potholes, materialistic mandates, demonic diversions, and the devil's deliberate deceptions. Mentees see the great benefit of accountability to someone else.

They know they will have to answer tough questions. They are guided by the knowledge that an account will be given for their behavior. Accountability is a great benefit!

Samuel and Saul shared a mentoring relationship. Samuel was the man of God who worked with King Saul the servant chosen to lead the nation of Israel.

The relationship began on a high note then tragically ended on a sad note. First Samuel chapters 9 through 15 detail their relationship.

Saul unfortunately allowed the enemy to derail and damage his relationship with his mentor. His behavior was brought into question when he gave account of his actions to his mentor Samuel.

Mentee accountability is a valuable benefit in heading off danger and staying on track from possible derailing diversions.

5. *Encouragement.*

Most of us would agree that *it's all about me* characterizes the philosophy of today's culture. What can you do for me rather than what can I do for you permeates the culture.

The Bible says a great deal about looking to meet the needs of others. Mentoring is a proactive way of making that happen. Mentors are cheerleaders for mentees.

They understand the role encouragement plays in lives of mentees. Mentees need encouragers. Mentors have learned the tremendous power and high-value of encouragement.

They know encouragement, is critical if mentees are to be motivated in positive, and uplifting ways.

Barnabas and Paul provide examples of this in the New Testament throughout the book of Acts 4:36-37, 9:36-36, 9:26-30, and 11:22-30. Encouragement is a great benefit to Mentees.

6. *Help in times of crisis.*

I've heard two things in life are certain, death and taxes. Those are in the equation for sure, but there are a number of other things that are also certain.

The Bible makes it clear that one of those things we will experience is trials and problems.

We don't know what they will be, when they will come, how long they will last, and how bad they will be, but we know they will come.

Mentors are towers of strength to lean on, shoulders of compassion to cry on, and pathfinders to follow when confronted with trials and difficulties on the road of life.

Mentors help mentees understand that God has purpose in what is happening with their lives. He chose the direction and details.

Mentors are trusted friends who provide counsel, comfort, and stability helping Mentees navigate through the stormy waters of trials, problems, and crises.

7. *Goal development and achievement.* Mentees receive valuable advice and objective input from mentors in developing personal goals.

They learn from their mentors to honestly evaluate their readiness to attempt each goal, think through long-term requirements necessary to reach each goal, and recognize the level of commitment necessary to reach each goal.

Mentees receive help with *monitoring their goals, suggested adjustments, council in removing impediments, gentle correction when sidetracked with other pursuits,* and *general guidance* to ensure successfully reaching their goals.

Mentors help Mentees *balance personal and spiritual growth*. They help them keep God as the central focus and priority of their lives.

Paul provides a great pattern of keeping the main thing the main thing with his instructions in his mentoring letters to Timothy in the New Testament.

8. *Wise counsel in life-impacting decisions.*

Mentees receive great benefit from knowledge and wise counsel of mentors. Mentors may be able to provide perspective, which mentees may not have considered.

They develop a depth of knowledge about mentees through the mentoring relationship that enables them to offer selected, sound, and solid advice on significant decisions.

Paul provides a great example of this in his dealings with Titus. A trusted advocate who can provide an objective viewpoint when weighing major life-impacting decisions is a tremendous personal benefit to mentees.

9. *Relationships with others are enhanced.*

Mentees who grow in their faith and pursue Christ-like lives, will positively impact every other relationship in their lives.

Family members, friends, fellow employees, business associates, neighbors, etc., will notice obvious changes in the lives of mentees. They will be impacted in positive ways because of these changes.

Those changes have the potential of producing even more changes in the lives of those people and relationships with the mentees. Changed lives of mentees have the potential of mending broken relationships.

God can use changed lives of mentees as the *Balm of Gilead* to help heal wounded souls. God can use mentees' changed lives to attract others to Christ. (Galatians 5:23-24)

10. *Enables Mentees to become mentors.*

Mentors were mentees before they became mentors. Their changed lives attract others as the Spirit of God begins to lay the groundwork for others to also be mentored.

God continually works in the hearts of mentees throughout their mentoring process. He plants seeds of desire to give back early in the process. These seeds develop, grow, and come to maturity as the mentoring cycle nears the finish line.

They come to understand the Lord of the harvest is looking for laborers to work in His fields. The harvest is not limited to gathering the fruit that someone else produced.

It involves planting, watering and nurturing their own crop. They come to realize they have a responsibility to invest in the lives of others because their mentors invested in them.

Becoming a mentor is one way of saying *yes* to God's command in Matthew 28:20 to *teach others to observe the things we've learned*. Mentees who become mentors have opportunities to give back by investing in the lives of others.

The ultimate goal of every mentor is to help mentees expand their personal and spiritual borders, realize their uniqueness and potential, and develop into mature Christians who will also become mentors.

Back to our story at Burger Chef

After returning home after my freshman year in college, I accepted an offer to return to my old job as night manager at Burger Chef for the summer.

My boss was going on vacation and wanted me to manage the store in his absence. He gave me instructions for the week and then said he had something important for me to attend to while he was gone.

He opened a box and pulled out two large brass valves and laid them on the desk. He began to describe what he wanted done. Burger Chef hamburgers were prepared through a chain broiler system cooked over gas burners inside the broiler unit.

Meat placed on a revolving chain moved through the broiler over the open flame and was deposited on the other end to be placed on sandwiches. Buns were toasted in the same way with a smaller burner.

Big John instructed me to change the two valves after the night shift on Monday, our slowest night. I was stunned for lack of a better word.

A number of thoughts came to mind. This could be dangerous. If I did something wrong I might blow up the building and me with it. I might install a valve incorrectly and disable the broiler that was the *bread and butter* of our business.

Could I do this? I didn't know how and this was certainly going to stretch me beyond my comfort zone.

Big John had mentored me as a manager when I stepped into the role at age 17. He'd brought me along at a good pace challenging me, instructing me and, teaching me to use my abilities.

This challenge would be different now.

With one valve in hand, he told me to follow him. We left his office for the back line where the broiler was located.

Big John began with a steady confident voice giving me step-by-step instructions on how to replace the old deteriorating valves with the pristine new ones.

The more he talked, the more confident I became. He finished his instructions by telling me he had great confidence in me and knew I could do it.

Monday night came. I managed the day shift and told my assistant night manager when he arrived to cover the night shift and that changing the valves was a go for later tonight. We'd talked earlier and made plans for him to assist me.

I arrived at 11:00 p.m. and in less than two hours we removed the old valves and replaced them with the new ones. The pipe sealer needed around eight hours to dry in order to seal the valves and prevent gas from leaking. We finished with a couple of hours to spare.

What does that story have to do with benefits to those who receive mentoring? Big John mentored me for over a year as the *big boss* and taught me a great deal about leading and managing.

He led me, stretched me, and challenged me to attempt bigger and better things. He helped me with achievable goals and provided step-by-step instructions on how to reach them.

I've drawn confidence and assurance a number of times from the goal I successfully achieved late one Burger Chef Monday night.

Mentees receive great benefits from mentors. They are enabled to accomplish bigger and greater things resulting from the mentoring process.

Hopefully this chapter helped you as a mentor appreciate the benefits you can help others receive.

Chapter 5

How do I Begin Mentoring?

The older more experienced fisherman provided fish for his small village on Slave Lake in the Northwest Territories of Canada. His demanding occupation earned him a fair living.

Daylight hours shorten greatly during the long winter months, which make fishing difficult and dangerous.

Temperatures often drop to forty-below-zero and lower after sundown and the lake is covered with thick ice for months. The experienced fisherman developed his fishing technique into an art.

He drilled holes in the ice at strategically located points across the lake and had the keen ability of finding and fishing them in the dark.

He placed anchored gill nets in the holes that stretched from the open hole to several feet below. He returned each day to check his nets, harvest the captured fish, and reset the nets for the next catch. The crusty ole fisherman followed this same routine for over 30 years.

He decided to employ a young man as his assistant. The young man arrived to begin his first day working in the ice fishing trade. The two men would return to the fish market headquarters after working twelve hours on the ice.

They double-checked their gear, and made sure they took along an extra five-gallon can of gasoline and mounted the two-man snowmobile.

The fiancée waited patiently for her young man to return safely. Twelve, thirteen, fifteen, seventeen hours passed and not a word. The outside temperature had dropped to -43 degrees.

Men can freeze to death on the ice in less than thirty minutes in those low temps. She was worried. Why hasn't she heard from her fiancée? Did something happen on the ice? Is he injured? Heaven forbid, could he be dead?

Did something happen to the men? Will they make it back alive? Stay with me until we reach the end of this chapter and I'll finish the rest of the story.

You may have heard it said the hardest part of most jobs is getting started. That is probably true for a number of jobs. Getting started in the role of mentoring doesn't have to be difficult. The key is knowing how to begin.

Jesus the great mentor used a simple approach that serves as a great pattern that we can emulate. Review Matthew 10:2-4, Mark 3:13-19 and Luke 6:12-16.

There are a number of chronological steps, which He took, that should make it easier for you to begin the role of mentor.

Getting Started – The Jesus Model

Jesus employed a simple mentoring strategy that changed men who then changed the world. His approach was well thought out, methodical, and step-by-step in scope.

Step 1 – PRAY.

You might think the admonition to pray is a given and you would be correct. Before the original 12 disciples were officially selected and ordained, Jesus removed Himself to a secluded place on a mountain. Luke 6:12 states that *Jesus went up on the mountain to pray, and He prayed all night.*

Why is this important? The magnitude of the moment cannot be overstated. Jesus, the Son of God, would soon pay the supreme sacrifice with His own blood to make the gift of salvation available to the whole world.

He was about to select men to whom He would entrust that precious gift. He needed men who would become church planters, organizers, leaders, and trainers of others to build His church that He would soon birth.

It was imperative that those selected be willing to receive mentoring preparation for their future use in the building of Christ's Church on the earth.

Mentors in the decision-making process of selecting mentees should spend time in prayer. Determining who may become good mentees is of paramount importance. Jesus prayed before selecting those He would mentor.

His mentees later became mentors and selected their own mentees who in turn became mentors, selecting their mentees and so on.

This cycle of mentees becoming mentors has continued from one generation to another and now rests with our generation.

Luke states that Jesus not only prayed, but He also informs us how long Jesus prayed. He prayed all night. He did not pray because of personal anxiety, fear, or worry.

He understood the value of enlisting His Father's guidance, grace, and blessing in the selections He was about to make. We need our heavenly father's guidance, grace, and blessing as we prayerfully choose our mentees.

Step 2 – SELECT someone to mentor.

Where should you look? Select someone from inside your circle of relationships. After praying and seeking God's guidance and direction, select the person God impresses you with.

Jesus selected twelve men after He gained peace through prayer concerning whom He should select. Verse 13 of chapter 6 of Luke recounts how Jesus gathered a number of people around Him and He selected twelve.

What made these twelve men different? These were the ones Jesus and His heavenly Father agreed on. Remember that He had already spoken to these men individually.

He said to one, *come, follow me and I will make you a fisher of men*. To another he said, *I saw you when you were under a tree*.

These twelve men were not strangers to Him or He a stranger to them. They were men already in established relationships with our Lord.

Jesus was confident that these men would be receptive to the instruction, guidance, i.e. mentoring that He would offer them.

We should select people with whom we have well-established relationships and are confident will be receptive to instruction, guidance, i.e. mentoring that we will offer them.

When you settle on a potential mentee candidate, arrange to meet with the individual. It may be best not to share the details of the subject and purpose of the meeting ahead of time.

Convey that you've been praying about something you'd like to share with them so they can pray with you about it. Let them know that you think it may be something that might be enjoyable and helpful for both of you.

Step 3 - MEET with mentee candidate.

Jesus met with the twelve men He selected to be His disciples/mentees. The Scripture doesn't reveal what was discussed in the meeting.

But I'm convinced Jesus approached each man individually. He informed them of their selection to become His disciple and His desire to pour His life into theirs.

Careful thought and planning should precede the first meeting with mentee candidates. Time, location, duration, content, and how the meeting will end should be carefully considered ahead of time.

Time – Agree on a day and time that works well for you and the potential mentee. Choose a date and time in the near future. Selecting a date in the extended future may lessen the interest of the potential mentee and could cause him to choose not to meet at all.

It would be wise to have a date and time in mind before contacting the potential mentee. I would discourage meeting the same day you contact the individual. The potential mentee might feel pressured and that you're moving too quickly in the process.

Location – The location of the meeting is important. Careful thought should be given to where you will meet.

The type of location should be considered carefully before an actual place is selected. Select a location with good atmosphere.

The meeting place should be quiet, relaxed, and comfortable. It should be an easy place to talk comfortably yet confidentially.

Choose light refreshment places rather than extending invitations for full meals. Remember, you will be there to meet not to eat.

Your time will be limited, so you want to get to the meat and potatoes of your reason for meeting without having to go through meat and potatoes on both your plates.

Choose a cup of coffee or soft drink and dessert. Local coffee shops like Starbucks, quiet restaurants with booths like Panera Bread, etc. are good examples of places I have personally used that work well.

Select a location convenient for both. The location of your first meeting could become the permanent location for the rest of your meetings.

Find a location that makes it easy on you and not a burden to your potential mentee.

Duration – The length of the meeting should be discussed and agreed on before the meeting occurs.

The initial meeting should last one hour or less. One-hour time frame is a good rule of thumb to apply to future meetings also.

Limiting the meeting to one hour accomplishes a number of things.

- *First*, the mentor and potential mentee both understand when the meeting will end.

- *Second*, both understand their time together is limited and they must keep moving forward in their discussion to complete the reason for meeting.

- *Third*, limiting the time to one hour will help stay on the subject at hand and discourage getting sidetracked with matters that can wait.

- *Fourth*, the one-hour format keeps the meeting from lasting too long. Long meetings may become fatiguing, lead to possible discouragement, leave a taste of dread for another meeting, and could cause the potential mentee to decline the invitation to be mentored.

Content – Mentors should adequately prepare in advance for the meeting.

Decide how to open the meeting. Be able to clearly state the purpose for the meeting. Set specific goals for the meeting.

Develop a game plan of items that will be discussed and in what order. Prepare printed materials to be shared. Consider how to end the meeting.

- *Start the Meeting* – A good way to begin the meeting is to reflect on the relationship shared with the candidate. Recount the qualities displayed by the candidate, which you've observed that make him a good choice as a mentee.

- *State the Purpose* – The individual's curiosity probably moved through a number of possible reasons why he was invited to the meeting. Move quickly to the reason for the meeting and state the purpose clearly.

- *Stick to your game plan*- Try to stay on track with the items you'd plan to discuss.

- *Share Printed Materials* – Prepared resource materials should be placed into the hands of candidates and explained. Instructions for examination and further reading should also be given.

Adjourn – Closing the meeting with the correct tone is important. Mentors should carefully think through how they will bring the meeting to a close. The mentee should clearly understand:

- Things that were discussed during the meeting.

- Future actions expected from him.

- Future steps that may take place.

- Commitment to be mentored should not be sought from the candidate at this meeting.

Step 4 – SECURE COMMITMENT by the mentee to be mentored.

Mentee candidates should not be asked to commit to mentorship during the introduction meeting.

Time elapsed between Jesus first meeting with His disciples prior to the mountain experience, and their eventual acceptance of Jesus' invitation.

Adequate time should be allowed by the mentor and agreed upon with the candidate for his decision.

The candidate should be encouraged to think about what will be required from him. He should be given time to pray about what decision he should make.

A minimum of two days and a maximum of one week is a good time frame to contemplate and make the decision.

Once the decision is made, respond appropriately. If the candidate commits to mentorship, be pro-active in scheduling the time and place for the next meeting.

If the candidate declines mentorship, thank him and assure him of your confidence and support. The conversation should end on a positive note regardless of the decision.

Step 5 – DETERMINE *tools* and *resources* to be used in the mentoring process.

Jesus had a plan for mentoring. He knew what He would teach the disciples. He taught them lesson by lesson for over three years.

Research and resource development should take place well in advance of the initial planning meeting with the mentor.

Mentors, before the initial planning meeting, should develop proposed goals for mentees. Specific, well-delineated goals should be written down and presented to mentees at the meeting.

Specific actions required of mentees should be defined and recorded. Details of each action are not crucial at this point.

Specific major actions should be listed, prioritized, and arranged in a systematic, chronological order. Actions will be expanded with inherent details during future meetings.

Step 6 – ADOPT a *mentoring plan*.

Jesus met with the twelve and helped them understand a little about what He was doing and hoped to do. That first meeting, when He commissioned them, was very important because it set the tone and framework for their future relationship.

Mentors should plan well for this meeting. This first meeting as mentor and mentee is crucial because it sets the tone and provides the framework for the future of the relationship. The theme of the meeting should be to define the direction of the mentoring relationship.

There are two important things to accomplish in this meeting; goals to strive for and expectations to be fulfilled by the mentor. These two things are paramount to success in the mentorship.

Mentees must know what they are hoping to achieve and what is expected of them.

Step 7 – MEET REGULARLY for a set period of time.

Little is mentioned in Scripture about the disciples' families and their personal lives at home. But we know they had families and responsibilities.

Jesus met with individuals, small groups, and with the entire group of 12 on occasions. He met regularly with His disciples.

Mentors should meet regularly with mentees. I would suggest once a week for 9-12 weeks.

These meetings should have one-hour time limits. Mentors should be time conscious and good timekeepers.

Once a month should be adequate after the initial 9-12 weeks is completed. Mentors should be constantly reflecting and evaluating progress of mentees.

Future meetings, content, needed actions, etc. should be guided by what has been learned.

Monthly meetings should be scheduled up to one year from the beginning of the mentoring relationship. Occasional phone calls are appropriate throughout the mentoring relationship. Emails and text messages are also appropriate.

The mentoring relationship never comes to a complete close. Hopefully, it will last a lifetime. Mentors should be interested in the continued progress, success and wellbeing of those they mentor for the rest of their lives.

Step 8 – MAKE each mentoring session *count*.

Jesus was the master at using time wisely. He took every opportunity and used each occasion to mentor His disciples.

He was always well prepared and knew what He wanted to accomplish with each lesson that He shared with His disciples/mentees.

Mentors should use their limited time with mentees wisely. They should come to meetings well prepared. They should know what they want to accomplish. Adequate time should be invested in developing lesson plans for these meetings.

Each lesson plan should contain the goal of the lesson to be learned, a simple explanation of the goal, resources to be used by the mentee, actions required for the mentee and the timeframe for completion.

Responsibility and accountability should be well defined to mentees. Mentors must do their best to help mentees understand what is expected. They should reinforce requirements to mentees with assured accountability.

Mentees should clearly understand they will be accountable for completion on learning tasks assigned them.

Trust, responsibility, and accountability are three pillars upon which the mentoring relationship rests.

Step 9 – INSPIRE mentees to *become* mentors.

The Scriptures clearly teach that Jesus' goal from the beginning of the mentoring process with His 12 disciples was to make them mentors.

He patiently and lovingly poured His life into theirs, preparing them also to pour their lives into others. They became mentors because the Great Mentor mentored them.

Mentors should remind themselves they are mentoring because they were mentored.

Their mentors invested time, talent, and treasure to play a role in the development of who they are today, the success they've enjoyed, and opportunities afforded to them.

They became mentors because of the confidence, training, and guidance of those who mentored them.

One goal of every mentor should be spiritual reproduction. They should take seriously the Apostle Paul's admonition to *train faithful men, who will become trainers of other faithful men.*

Mentors should plant seeds of future mentors in the fertile soil of the mentoring relationship with mentees early in the mentoring process. These seeds should be fertilized, cultivated, watered, and pruned throughout the mentoring process.

Those seeds will become strong, well-developed plants by the end of the mentoring process. Mentors should cast a vision for future spiritual reproduction in mentees throughout the process that will produce the future fruit of new mentors.

Step 10 - HELP your mentee *find* his *first* mentee.

The metamorphosis from mentee to mentor is rewarding to watch. It's a great joy for mentors to observe mentees develop mentor wings, contemplate flying alone, and leave the security of their mentor's watch care, test their wings for the first time, gain confidence, and eventually soar to heights they never dreamed possible.

Mark 6:7 records Christ *sending out* the disciples by twos in order to accomplish great things. He'd been training them for that purpose.

He wanted them to become *spiritual reproducers*. Mentors should be planning for this moment from the beginning of the mentoring relationship. The ultimate goal is to prepare mentees to become mentors.

Care should be taken in guiding these new mentors in the selection of their first mentees. A checklist of steps in mentee selection should be created for these new mentors.

Walking them through the process of making good selections is essential. This will be their first attempt at mentoring. One final part of mentoring is helping them make a good choice of their first mentee.

Encourage them to keep in close contact throughout the selection process. Make available to them your knowledge, wisdom, and help. Let them know you are there for them when they need you.

Step 11 - COMMISSION New Mentors.

Mentees, having completed their mentorship journey, are ready to become mentors. They have selected someone they would like to mentor. They are now ready to begin mentoring.

Jesus' final act before returning to Heaven after His resurrection was to commission His disciples to teach others what they had learned, according to Matthew 28:18 – 20. The final act of good mentors is to commission mentees.

Mentors should remind mentees what has been learned, what their responsibilities are, and that great confidence has been placed in them. Mentors should help mentees believe they will be successful in mentoring others.

Mentors should relate the same reassurance that Jesus left with His disciples. Jesus told His disciples in Matthew 28 that He would be with them the rest of their lives.

He would be with them wherever they went in the world. Mentors should reassure these new mentors they are available to help in their mentoring journey.

Mentors should offer themselves as a resource to these new mentors during their first attempt at mentoring others. They should carefully balance their offer to help with granting independence to their former mentees.

Now back to our story of the fisherman on Slave Lake.

The young man and older experienced fishermen have been missing for almost 24 hours. The temperature had dropped to -43 below zero.

No one had heard from or seen them. The young man's fiancée was worried sick. The older fisherman's business partner was concerned also.

What could have happened to these two fishermen? The decision was made to form search parties and scour the frozen lake in an all-out search and rescue effort.

The community was mobilized. The lake was divided into specific grid areas to be searched. The search began.

About two hours into the search, one lone man on his snowmobile spotted a small light in the distant darkness. Could it be them? He tightened his grip on the throttle and the snowmobile sped forward full speed ahead.

The flickering light grew brighter. The darkness gave way to two men waving their arms in an attempt to signal the approaching snowmobile.

The men had been found! A radio message was sent to a rescue unit and within 30 minutes the men were rescued.

The older fisherman described what had transpired that left them stranded on the ice. He explained that a mistake had been made when gathering their gear in preparation for the fishing trip.

After completing the record catch of fish, they began their journey back across the ice and home.

Their gas gauge indicated their fuel level was low. They stopped on the ice, removed their gas cap, and proceeded to pour in 5 gallons of gasoline they'd brought along.

They replaced the gas cap and started the engine. They moved forward about 20 feet and the engine stopped working. They couldn't get the engine started.

They investigated possible reasons for the engine's failure and made a frightening discovery.

They mistakenly brought the wrong gas can. Instead of 5 gallons of gasoline, they brought a 5-gallon can of diesel fuel.

When they stopped on the ice, they filled the gas tank with what they thought was gas. The gasoline engine would not work with diesel fuel.

They were stranded miles from home and many degrees below zero with the real possibility of dying in the darkness. Their innocent mistake could've had horrible consequences.

Following the proper model of mentoring provides a great resource for success. Failing to gather the proper resources or taking anything for granted could have unintended negative consequences.

Careful planning and preparation are absolutely necessary for mentors. Nothing must be left to chance. They must be willing to invest their time and resources into the lives of those they mentor.

Jesus provides a great model for mentors to follow. Following this step-by-step process in the mentoring of others has the great potential of spiritual reproduction of more mentors.

Follow the Jesus model, you can't go wrong.

CHAPTER 6

Let the Mentoring Begin.

The poor old man had spiraled down to rock bottom since losing his sight five years ago. He had no family, no money, no place to live, and no means to help himself financially. His pride was completely gone. He was hungry and desperate.

He rummaged through a dumpster, found a piece of cardboard, and scribbled in barely legible script *I'm blind please help*. He found a tin can and quickly wiped it as clean as possible with a used paper towel.

He hoped someone would have pity on him and drop in some loose change or anything that might help him.

The old man had grown up in this large metropolitan city. He could find his way around even in the dark of his blindness. He made his way to a busy street corner with his new sign and tin can.

A multitude of sighted people turned a blind eye to this man without sight. No one seemed to notice him. Not one person recognized or seemed to care about his destitute condition.

A well-dressed gentleman approached the blind man and immediately sensed his need of help. He evaluated the poor man's situation.

The gentleman was the CEO of a large corporation based in this city. He quickly arrived at a possible solution for this poor man's situation.

What could be a possible solution to improve the poor blind man's circumstances? What would the CEO suggest and do that might make a difference in this man's life? We'll find out when we finish the story at the end of this chapter.

Dr. Richard J. Krejcir in *Tips for a Successful Discipleship and Mentoring*, provides great suggestions on basic things for mentors to remember. http://www.discipleshiptools.org

The most important thing to remember is obedience to the principles of the Word of God. This includes but is not limited to faithful practice of the spiritual disciplines.

Mentors cannot be affective in nurturing others if they are not spiritually healthy themselves.

Bible study, prayer, faithful church attendance, personal and corporate worship and faithful stewardship giving should be the consistent prior practice of mentors and characterize their life style during and after the mentoring relationship.

Healthy interpersonal relationships should characterize mentors as they open the doors of their lives to mentees. Good relationships with spouses, children, other relatives, coworkers, church members etc., enhance mentors ability to inspire and nurture mentees.

Mentors should keep some things in mind as they open the door to new mentoring relationships.

- Remaining in an attitude of prayer, keeping a good sense of humor, and being sensitive to others are paramount.

- Be prepared when meeting with mentees.

- Be on time.

- Introduce the subject and text and provide background.

- Stay on the subject and help mentees stay on the subject.

- The meeting should convey an atmosphere of safety for asking questions, providing encouragement, love, care, and safe vulnerability.

- Lead the discussion but do not dominate it.

- Good questions can help mentees respond well to the subject or passage and aid in better understanding of passages or principles.

- Mentors should challenge mentees to think on deeper levels, to discover a concept or principle, understand what it means, how they can be changed because of it, and how to apply it to their lives.

- Mentors should be excited when mentees make progress in growing and give affirmation to their efforts.

- Mentors should search for ways to inspire mentees. Sharing mentor's personal life stories is one way to help mentees discover and apply precepts and principles of God's Word.

- Do not be afraid to discuss important real-life struggles while carefully applying appropriate biblical principles.

- Do not be afraid to deviate from the planned subject of the week to address a current crisis or stress that mentees may be going through. Let the Holy Spirit be your guide.

- Start on time and end on time. Mentors communicate to mentees that their time is important by beginning and ending on time.

- Be open, sensitive, and flexible to making changes in your approach and format as needs arise.

- Mentors must be interested in the lives of mentees and convey that interest to them.

- Allowing mentees to express their ideas and views conveys respect and love toward them.

- Mentors must remember that every meeting may not be a complete success. There will be setbacks and sometimes discouragement. Keep in mind the big picture, which has produced many successes. Do not allow discouragement to takeover.

- Mentors should remember that planned material might not be completely covered in each session. Do not be handcuffed by feeling that everything must be covered. Resume the material in the next meeting if necessary or simply move on to the next principle.

- Do not be afraid to address faulty or heretical positions of mentees. Be kind and not condescending but with love point out the error.

- Keep your sense of humor. Laugh and balance humor and seriousness during mentoring sessions.

- Mentors should lead mentees in developing an attitude of prayer throughout the week prior to their meetings, during their meetings, and after their meetings.

Now back to our story about the poor blind man.

The poor blind man was destitute with no means of support. He'd been sitting on the busy street corner for hours with nothing to show for his time or money to buy something to eat.

The CEO stopped and analyzed the situation. He had compassion for the man and realized the man needed help.

What could he do? There were a number of choices that he could make. He could drop some money into the tin can that would help the man but only a little. He could ignore the situation and just walk on by and do nothing. He chose neither of these.

He asked permission from the blind man to look at his sign. He picked up the sign up and turned it over.

He took a large felt tip marker from his pocket and quickly scribbled something on the blank backside of the sign. He handed the sign back to the blind man and went on his way.

Immediately people passing by began dropping money into his once empty tin can. In a matter of minutes the can was overflowing. The poor blind man could hardly believe what happened.

He removed the money from the can stuffed it in his pockets placing the once again empty can on the ground in front of the sign. Money filled the can quickly the second time also.

The blind man could hardly believe his good fortune but he knew it must have something to do with what was written on the sign. So he asked a passerby to read him the message written on the sign.

Do you remember what the blind man had scribbled in blind script originally on the sign? *Blind – need help*. The sign now read: *It's a beautiful day. You can see it, I can't!*

I'm sure you can see the difference in the message. What's the point of the illustration? The blind man could not see past the problems of his situation.

The CEO saw a way to positively impact the blind man's situation. His expertise, experience and energy helped to improve the blind man's life.

Mentors may not necessarily be CEOs of large companies, but they do have potential to impact in positive ways their mentees.

Mentees often cannot see past their shortcomings and fail to see their potential. Mentors bring their expertise, experience, and energy in helping mentees find and achieve their potential.

Mentors spend more than a just a couple of minutes with mentees throughout the mentoring process. They do more than scribble on the back of cardboard signs.

Their mentoring sessions are personal and spiritual building blocks in the maturing process of mentees.

Care should be taken in preparation, participation, and presentation for mentoring meetings. So let's get on with it. Get busy mentoring!

CHAPTER 7

Stop, Look, Listen

A man feared his wife wasn't hearing as well as she used to and thought she might need a hearing aid. Not quite sure how to approach her, he called the family doctor to discuss the problem.

The doctor told him there is a simple informal test the husband could perform to give the doctor a better idea about her hearing loss.

"Here's what you do," said the doctor, "stand about 40 feet away from her, and in a normal conversational speaking tone see if she hears you. If not, go to 30 feet, then 20 feet, and so on until you get a response."

That evening, the wife was in the kitchen cooking dinner, and the husband was in the den. He thought, let's give this a try.

So standing about 40 feet away he... At the end of the chapter we'll find out what he did and if it was successful.

Being a good listener is important for the mentor and mentee. The old expression; *stop, look,* and *listen* before crossing streets is valid for mentoring also. Successful mentors learn quickly the value and importance of being good listeners.

Listening with perceptive ears may help mentors gain broader understanding of mentees. It can open the door for mentees to share successes and failures and enable mentors to discover mentee strengths, weaknesses, and areas that may need further exploration.

Mentor Listening Reminders

1. Make and **maintain eye contact**. There are a number of things that take place when making eye contact.

- *Shows Respect*. In most Western countries including the United States, eye contact shows respect. Respect is afforded to mentees and earned by mentors through eye contact. Eye contact indicates a level of equal importance between people.

Mentors may gain important insights from reactions and emotions flowing through mentees' eyes. Equally important, mentors' compassion and sincerity will be conveyed through eye contact. Eye contact helps both parties maintain confidence that they are on the same page.

• *Shows interest*. Looking down or away from mentees conveys a message of disinterest or minimizes the importance of what mentees may be saying.

Look mentees in the eyes, smile and nod approvingly from time to time. This will convey your interest as a respectful authoritative figure and affirm the strong bond that you share.

• *Shows affirmation*. Maintaining eye contact when bestowing praise on mentees conveys the strong feeling of affirmation. Mentees not only hear what is being said but they also read the retina message beamed from the mentor's eyes.

Affirmation and appreciation through eye contact build connection in the relationship.

• *Shows understanding*. Eye contact is one of the most intimate forms of communication. Mentors gain assurance that what they are saying is being understood.

This enables them to continue with the next thought after confirmation through eye contact that both parties understand previous steps.

Eye contact is something that most people do not think about. Children should be taught at a young age to look people in the eye when they're talking to them.

Failure to learn this critical communication skill could hinder them later in life. Learning this can help develop, maintain, and project a positive image, which may aid them with life-changing pursuits.

2. Provide **auditory feedback**. You may ask *what you mean by that.* Good mentors understand the need to be supportive while mentees share feelings.

Auditory feedback simply means to sincerely and in interesting ways encourage mentees to continue what they are saying reassuring them they are being listened to.

Yes, no, oh, really, I see, hum, mm, is that right, wow, and *my, my,* are a few examples of auditory feedback that when strategically interjected in the conversation will encourage mentees to continue.

3. Be aware of your **body language**. Body language is more important than some may realize. Good body language displayed by mentors, aid mentees in feeling relaxed and comfortable during mentoring sessions.

Many resources are available that describe in detail the art of displaying good body language. I will mention a few to remember.

• *Uncrossed arms* indicate that you are open and not defensive to what is being said by mentees.

• *Facing and looking* at mentees indicates that you are giving them your undivided attention. This enhances their value and elevates the importance of what is being discussed.

• *Nodding your head* from time to time reassures mentees that you are listening to what they are saying and intently interested in it.

• *Smiling* at appropriate moments brings warmth to the conversation.

• Serious *facial expressions* convey to mentees that you understand the seriousness and importance of what they are telling you.

• *Body movements* should be calculated. Shifting from side to side, crossing and uncrossing legs repeatedly, crossing and uncrossing arms, looking out the window or at the door etc., may be misunderstood by mentees.

This may be perceived as showing disinterest in what is being said and as unimportant to the mentor. It may appear that the mentor is in a hurry and has more important things to do.

• Care should be taken with *physical contact*. A handshake or pat on the back is an appropriate physical form of greeting and encouragement.

4. **Stay focused**. Mentees will sense if you have your mind on something else or if you are fully engaged in the moment with them.

Mentors should constantly double-check to make sure they stay focused on what mentees are saying to them.

If mentees believe you are focused on them and what they are telling you, they will be at ease with taking whatever time is necessary to continue with what they would like to say.

One sign to look for is mentees rushing through what they are saying. This may indicate they have the impression that you are not focused on them or what they are saying.

Remaining focused and fully engaged enables mentees to feel supported and truly the center of attention. This encourages them to freely share their feelings and what is happening in their lives.

5. Be careful **not to interrupt** at inopportune moments. Remember the 80/20 rule of being a good listener.

Good mentors will remain silent and listen to 80% of what mentees are saying and only interject 20% or less with their own words during that part of the conversation.

Interruptions should be brief with support for what is being said and suggestive words encouraging more to be said.

A few examples; *that's really interesting, that is really neat, please continue, I'd like to hear more about that, that's great can you expand on it a little more, that's heading in the right direction,* etc.

6. **Repeat** what you've heard. Mentors should repeat what mentees say from time to time during the conversation. This accomplishes two things.

- Mentees are reassured you are listening to what they are saying.

- It ensures you correctly understand what is being said.

Here are a few examples; *so you're saying, so this happened last week, and you've felt this way for a while, and you tried this before, so you feel like you failed, so you feel like this was a great success, etc.*

7. Be careful about **finishing sentences** for mentees. Helping mentees by supplying words or finishing their sentences should be done carefully and only at appropriate times.

Moving too quickly may cause mentees to feel rushed or pressured. It may distract from their train of thought and make the next words more difficult to call to mind and speak.

Mentors should be perceptive in recognizing when mentees are struggling for words and help them with suggested words to complete their thoughts and sentences. This should always be done with a suggested question.

Supply the words as though they are a question as you finish the sentence. This approach allows mentees to affirm that you have correctly understood what they mean.

This approach allows mentees to clarify your understanding of what they meant to say.

8. Limit **focusing on yourself**. Mentors should be careful when offering personal examples and illustrations. Personal experiences can be used to reinforce and support what mentees are saying.

Care should be taken not to use personal examples that may unintentionally cause mentees to lose focus on what they are trying to say. This can result in drawing attention to you as a mentor and cause focus on the topic of discussion to be lost.

Avoid long drawn out illustrations. When personal illustrations are used, they should be direct, short, and to the point. Effort should be made to apply illustrations undergirding the validity of what mentees are saying.

9. **Ask appropriate questions**. A more in-depth discussion of the art and content of good questions will be covered in a later chapter.

Mentors, who are listening well, will ask thoughtful questions that encourage mentees to open up and give more details about the topic of discussion.

10. **Relate** to what you're hearing. Mentees share emotions and feelings during mentoring sessions. Mentors who listen well, relay back to mentees accurate recognition of expressed emotions and feelings. This conveys genuine empathy and compassion to mentees from their mentors.

Back to our Story

Let's review our story for a moment. The husband was concerned about his wife's hearing. He thought she was having a problem with her hearing.

He called his doctor and to ask him what he might do to find out without embarrassing her.

The doctor told him stand 40 feet away and talk in a normal voice to see if she could hear you. If she did not answer, move to 30 feet, 20 feet, and 10 feet until she responded.

That evening, the wife was in the kitchen cooking dinner and he was in the den. He thought to himself. She's about 40 feet away; let's give this a try.

Then in a normal tone he asked, "Honey, what's for dinner?"

No response.

So he moved closer to the kitchen, about 30 feet from his wife and repeated, "Honey, what's for dinner?" still no response.

Next he moved into the dining room about 20 feet from his wife and asked, "Honey, what's for dinner?" He received no response.

He walked up to the kitchen door, about 10 feet away. "Honey, what's for dinner?" No response.

So he walked right up behind her and in a loud voice said: "Honey, what's for dinner?"

Finally his wife yelled out: "James, for the FIFTH time I said, FRIED CHICKEN!"

Moral of the story: We may be so busy talking that we do not hear what needs to be heard. To be good mentors we must become good listeners.

CHAPTER 8

Good Questions

Good Mentoring

The art of asking good questions can be as challenging as being a good listener.

Irene Leonard makes a good point when she says, *"Asking good questions is productive, positive, creative, and can get us what we want."*

Most people believe this to be true and yet people do not ask enough good questions. Perhaps one of the reasons is that effective questioning requires it be combined with effective listening.

Here are some things to remember about asking questions when mentoring.

1. **Ask appropriate questions**. Consider the depth of commitment and trust within your relationship. Ask questions that are appropriate to the depth.

Prying too deeply at the beginning will not work. Conversely, if you are asking superficial questions after you have been meeting for a significant time, your meetings will become bland.

Try to gently guide the relationship forward in each session. Let your questions slowly grow toward vulnerability and openness.

2. **Ask focused questions**. Get to the heart of the issue being explored.

3. **Ask open-ended questions**. Encourage discussion. Questions that simply fill in the blank, or can be answered by "yes" or "no," will not lead anywhere.

4. **Ask moderate questions**. Asking for superlatives creates unnecessary anxiety on the mentee. For example, instead of asking what was the best, most significant,

most meaningful event in your childhood? Ask, what was a good, meaningful, or significant event?

5. **Ask clarifying questions**. Give your mentee the opportunity to restate what he has said so that you might grasp more fully his intent. Encourage him to explain why he thinks what he does, or what brought him to that conclusion.

6. **Ask effective questions**. Effective questions are powerful and can be thought provoking.

a. Effective questions are *open-ended* and not leading questions.

b. Effective questions are *what or how* questions.

c. Effective questions are not *why* questions. Why questions can make people defensive so care should be taken in using them.

d. Effective questions always wait for an answer.

Here are some examples of questions that might be helpful in the mentoring process.

1. Identification Questions

a. How do you feel about this?

b. What concerns you most?

c. What seems to be the problem with this?

d. What seems to be holding you back?

    e. What do you think about trying this?

2. Questions for more Information

    a. What do you mean by that?

    b. Please tell me more?

    c. What else?

    d. How successful has this been for you?

    e. What is your plan for accomplishing this?

    f. How would you handle this?

    g. What do you really want?

3. Action Questions

    a. What are you going to do?
    b. When will you do it?

    c. When do you hope to finish?

    d. What is your first step?

    e. What is the next step?

John Mallison Ministries has a great list of questions for mentors to ask mentees in identifying their needs and direction for the future.

1. **Developing long-term objectives**.

    a. Where do you want your life to be in five to ten

years?

    b. What do you think will be required to get there?

    c. What do you see as hindering you from getting there?

    d. What will help you?

2. **Basic areas of life.** (Questions about friendships, marriage, family, spiritual life, ministry, work, involvement in the community, etc.)

    a. Where do you need to grow?

    b. Do you have some chronic problem areas?

    c. What are they?

    d. Where are you experiencing repeated failures?

    e. Where do you feel inadequate?

3. **Positive impact questions for future growth.**

    a. What attitudes or values do you feel the need to cultivate?

    b. What habits and behaviors are you trying to establish or change?

    c. In what ways do you want to increase your knowledge and understanding?

CHAPTER 9

Successful Mentoring Meetings

Wise planning in advance of mentoring sessions will enable more productive meetings and the best use of time for *all* involved. A key component of wise planning is developing a basic framework for the meeting.

An agenda should be developed that will effectively keep the meeting on track. Here are five key elements that will help mentoring meetings be successful.

In my early days as a leader, I developed a five-step approach to cover these key elements that has worked effectively for me.

Mentors should remember that agendas are merely guides and not set in stone.

Agendas should be strong enough to keep the meeting on track, but flexible enough to allow deviation when situations or specific instances require changes.

Element One - *Examination*

The first step is gathering information that will be helpful throughout the meeting. Basic greetings and amenities should be passed between mentors and mentees.

These opening moments are important because they provide information about what is going on in mentee's lives and how they may be doing emotionally, physically, and spiritually.

Asking good questions during the opening moments and making and maintaining eye contact will urge mentees to openly share what's happening in their lives.

Examples of good questions one might ask are: *How are things going? Tell me about your week. Is there anything you'd like to share? How are things going at work? Are you doing well physically? How is your family?*

Carefully listening while maintaining eye contact will aid mentors in discerning what direction the meeting should take. There may be a specific incident or situation that will require refocusing from the intended topic set for the meeting.

Be flexible and not afraid to refocus on the incident or situation. Mentees may need special help and guidance to understand, confront, and conquer this new challenge.

This new challenge may provide a teachable moment for mentees. Mentors should recognize this whole scenario as a vital part of mentoring.

Review assigned tasks from previous meetings.

Element Two - *Evaluation*

The second step in the meeting is assessment of the information learned during the first step or part of the meeting. What should be focused on?

- The *first area* of evaluation or assessment is *taking stock of what the mentee just shared*. Is there something that should be explored further? Was something mentioned that brought up a red flag of concern?

- The *second area* to be evaluated is *assessing how well he's fulfilled his obligations assigned in the previous meeting*. Accountability is an important part of the mentoring process.

Mentees should be taught early that they are expected to fulfill assigned tasks and will give an account concerning their efforts. During the evaluation part of the meeting, mentors should review aloud with mentees the tasks that were assigned during the previous meeting.

This should be done one task at a time, allowing a response from mentees on the status of each task.

Care should be taken to allow mentees to express their successes and failures at task completion. Additional information seeking questions or suggested words to elaborate further, will help mentors better evaluate their progress in these areas.

- A *third area* of evaluation is *gut feelings of how well mentees are progressing*. This should be a comprehensive look based on cumulative information gained by mentors.

Mentors will be able to tell quickly if the mentoring relationship is going to work. This is based on the level of commitment of mentees, their willingness to receive guidance and instruction, and their ability to achieve success in the process.

Accurate evaluation requires adequate and pertinent information. Mentors must pay careful attention to what mentees may be communicating early in the meeting during the examination phase. Good evaluation is key in determining the direction for the rest of the meeting.

Element Three - *Obligation*

The third step in the mentoring meeting is to assign tasks for the next meeting. Mentees should understand what is expected of them, the time frame for its completion, and the expected outcomes.

- *Assigning busywork* should be avoided. Only meaningful tasks that will help mentees stretch themselves and grow should be assigned.

- *Obligating mentees* with the expectation of accountability provides a framework that will reach beyond the tasks assigned during the mentoring process.

- *Determining task assignment* should be based on a couple of things.

o First - Tasks that were assigned at previous meetings, which have not yet successfully been fulfilled, should be reconsidered and possibly reassigned again.

Much can be learned from not completing a task that was assigned. This is a teachable moment and should not be overlooked by mentors. Suggestions will be shared later in this chapter.

o Second - New tasks may or may not be appropriate for the next meeting.

When mentees have made adequate progress, then assigning a new task may be in order. New task assignments should be based on previous progress and future goals. These tasks should be well thought out by mentors before the meeting.

Tasks should be part of an overall strategy of growth by mentors for mentees. New tasks should be built upon the foundation of successfully completed tasks. These new tasks should be within the ability of mentees.

- There are three things that mentors should remember when assigning specific tasks to mentees.

o Tasks should be well defined with simple instructions and specific expectations. Mentees should leave the meeting knowing exactly what they are expected to do.

o Mentees and mentors should agree on a timeframe for task completion. The date for completion should be determined for each task. Declaring deadlines will elevate the importance of tasks and help mentees make them a higher priority.

o Mentees should be reminded that accountability is required for the tasks that are being assigned. If they understand up front that they will be asked to report on their efforts, this will serve as a motivator to keep on track to fulfill the required task.

The fact that they will be accountable may encourage them to push forward rather than procrastinate and pull back.

Element Four - *Allocation*

Allocation is the fourth element or step that will help mentoring meetings be more meaningful and successful. The word allocation literally means *distribute* or *share*.

These two synonyms for the word allocation described different aspects of what should be given to mentees during mentoring meetings.

• *Share* - This aspect refers to verbally sharing with mentees; honest evaluation, constructive criticism, and positive steps to move forward. Specific tasks agreed upon earlier in the meeting require concrete verbal steps to take in order to accomplish those tasks.

Mentors should not only be specific with the assignment of tasks, setting appropriate timeframe deadlines, but they should also provide instructions on how to test what may be accomplished by mentees. The *how* of accomplishment for mentees is very important!

• *Distribute* – Mentors should spend time preparing materials to place in the hands of their mentees. Helpful resources should be researched, reproduced, and placed into mentees' hands.

Content should be guided by the subject matter to be discussed, personal and spiritual goals to be achieved, growth in the spiritual disciplines, immediate family relationships, and zeroing in on weak areas that need strengthening.

Element Five – *Affirmation*

The fifth step in the meeting is *affirmation*. Affirmation has an interesting definition. There are at least ten words that could be easily and accurately substituted for affirmation.

I've selected a few of these to define how the meeting should be brought to a close.

• The first word is *declaration*. Mentors remember that mentees need to know they are making progress. Mentors should say things like *I'm very pleased with the way things are moving along. You're making great progress.*

Mention one specific area of improvement. By doing this, mentors are declaring they recognize and appreciate the effort of mentees.

• A second word found in the definition of affirmation is *confirmation*. Mentors seek to confirm and reassure mentees that they are and will be successful.

Mentees need *confirmation* that they are doing well and all their hard work is paying off. They need the approval of their mentors. They need it confirmed in their minds.

• *Support* is the third word found in the definition of affirmation. Each mentoring meeting should add another brick in building the *support* wall for mentees.

They should be made to feel that mentors are going to be there for them. Mentors should convey words and deeds that reinforce their support. Providing a *safety net of support* encourages mentees to launch beyond their comfort zones to attempt greater things.

Affirmation reinforces personal value and validates efforts for improvement. *Affirmation* helps end the meeting on a positive note. This is important because it will help motivate mentees to continue the process, provide them with encouragement, and set the tone for the next meeting.

Examination, Evaluation, Obligation, Allocation, and *Affirmation* provide a great framework for developing an agenda and guide for successful mentoring meetings.

CHAPTER 10

Spiritual Disciplines

There were two lumberjacks and one was much older than the other. The younger of the two was proud of the fact that he could chop down a certain number of trees quicker than the older lumberjack.

The older lumberjack was known for his speed. He challenged the younger one to help him learn a valuable lesson. The he proposed a contest to see who could cut down the most trees in one day.

They began. The younger man chopped down one tree after another and would not stop. He was determined. He knew the contest looked promising in his favor when he noticed the older lumberjack would chop for only one hour then take a fifteen-minute rest.

Which one do you think cut down the most trees at the end of the day and won the contest? Why? We'll find out at the end of the chapter.

Growth and development of mentees and the *spiritual disciplines* are inseparable. Christian mentors understand the value and necessity of challenging mentees to work hard in developing spiritual disciplines in their personal lives.

They must impress mentees with the value and necessity of developing spiritual disciplines.

What are spiritual disciplines? The short version is an *intentional effort to develop intimacy with God with the goal of living authentic spiritual lives*.

They are called disciplines because they are not natural things we do. Physical disciplines include developmental exercises within the natural order of the physical body or mental aptitudes.

Spiritual disciplines are developmental exercises that open the door to the spiritual realm of existence. They are disciplines because we must make a conscious choice to engage in them.

There are times when we do not feel like doing what we know is necessary for good spiritual health. Disciplines provide methodology, structure, and order to carry us through those times we would otherwise ignore our spiritual health.

This chapter will introduce the area commonly known as spiritual disciplines.

Developing spiritual disciplines requires genuine effort and hard work with the promise of rewards.

AuthenticDiscipleship.org http://www.authenticdiscipleship.org offers a great chapter introducing spiritual disciplines.

I'll build upon some of the thoughts contained in that chapter.

What are some requirements of the spiritual disciplines?

- A spiritual discipline requires *deliberately imposing a habit* that nurtures spiritual health and fosters spiritual growth.

- A spiritual discipline requires *deliberately imposing actions* that alter existing life and thought patterns resulting in breaking the normal cycle of life. The result is refocusing from the mundane to the potential of becoming exceptional.

- Spiritual discipline requires a *repeated action* dictated by a spiritual decision *rather than reacting* to environment and circumstances.

- A spiritual discipline requires *developing spiritual patterns* by engaging in spiritual exercises with the goal of intimacy with God.

What are some rewards provided through spiritual disciplines?

- *Spiritually maturing* as a Christian is one great reward earned through engaging in spiritual disciplines.

- Intimacy with God is another great reward.

- Mentees may see their spiritual lives elevated from ordinary to extraordinary!

Now let's finish the story about the two lumberjacks.

One was quite older than the other. And the younger lumberjack was somewhat proud of the fact that he could chop down a certain number of trees quicker than the older lumberjack.

Even though the older lumberjack was known for his speed, he felt an urge to challenge the younger one. So he proposed a challenge to see who could cut down the most trees in one day.

They began, and the younger man was chopping down one after another and would not stop, he was determined.

He knew it looked promising when he noticed the older lumberjack chopping for only one hour then taking a fifteen-minute rest.

But when the end of the day came the older lumberjack had cut down 1/3 more trees than the younger lumberjack.

Somewhat miffed the younger man asked him how was it possible that the older man cut more than him especially after taking breaks all day long.

I didn't take a single break and cut furiously all day. ☐The older lumberjack said, "it's quite simple, every time I stopped and sat down, I not only rested, I also sharpened my axe."

The spiritual disciplines continually keep the Christian's spiritual axe sharp. Developing them will enable mentees to grow, mature, and be successful over the long haul.

We could look at several things that might qualify as spiritual disciplines. There are many lists available from a plethora of sources with a variety of suggested spiritual disciplines.

Obviously all cannot be covered in this book. I've selected a few that we'll discuss in the next two chapters. Mentors are encouraged to research, expand, and develop their own lists based on needs of individual mentees.

CHAPTER 11

Internal

Spiritual Disciplines

In ancient Greece, Socrates held knowledge in high esteem. One day an acquaintance said to the great philosopher, "Do you know what I just heard about your friend?"

"Hold on a minute," Socrates replied. "Before you tell me anything I'd like you to pass a little test. It's called the Triple Filter Test." "Triple Filter Test" the man asked?

"That's right," Socrates continued. "Before you talk to me about my friend, it might be a good idea to take a moment and filter what you're going to say. That's why I call it the triple filter test."

Socrates began to administer the test by asking him three questions. The questions are sound questions and appropriate for every Christian to ask today.

At the end of the chapter we'll look at the questions and his answers and how they impact the quest for internal spiritual disciplines.

The internal spiritual discipline of *prayer* is a good place to begin. Most of us would agree that the Bible has much to say about the need of prayer in every Christian's life.

Jesus set the example by often slipping away to quiet and private places to pray, Luke 5:15-16. There are a number of passages in Scripture we could look at, Colossians 4:2, and Acts 6:4.

Prayer is a spiritual discipline for a number of reasons.

- Prayer is the way God chose to *provide our access* into His presence. While in His presence, we encounter Him personally and receive comfort, strength, and direction.

- Prayer *shifts our focus* from the temporal to the eternal.

- Prayer *broadens our scope* and helps us gain better understanding of God's bigger picture in His plan and our role in that plan.

- Prayer helps us *move beyond our limited understanding* into God's deeper meaning of truth and life.

- Prayer is *transformational*! It makes us keenly aware of our status as children of God, challenges us to be more like Jesus, and humbles our hearts enabling God to use us for His purposes.

The **study of God's word** is an important internal spiritual discipline. Emotional experiences though delightful will not free our hearts nor strengthen our minds.

Jesus taught that truth is what opens the door to freedom. Study empowers the disciplining and steadying of the mind through developing knowledge and wisdom.

Knowing the truth is foundational for the disciple and sets him on the path for freedom.

The Bible addresses this important discipline and a number of passages, Second Timothy 2:15, and Romans 12:1-2 come to mind.

- What is a good way to *define study* as a spiritual discipline?

   o It is a means of knowing God and learning His truths and priorities through the study of Scripture.

   o When you love someone, you want to know all you can about him. It is a means of becoming closer to them. Knowing about God is a way of falling more deeply in love with Him.

107

o Contemplation is devotional, meditation is developmental, but study is analytical.

o Bible study may be a combination of things:

- Regular reading of Scripture.

- Learning the shape of redemptive history.

- Book studies to become familiar with how a particular book falls into the plan of redemption.

- Topical studies to answer burning questions in your mind or heart.

- Verse studies to focus on a particular aspect of God's truth that caught your attention.

• Why would you *incorporate study* as a discipline into your life?

o All the disciplines are a means for the Holy Spirit to transform us. *Be transformed by the renewing of your mind*. It is a way of encouraging the transformation God has started within.

o It is not enough to believe the truth we've heard from someone else. It necessitates exploration to see and learn the truth for ourselves.

o In making the truth my own, not only am I transformed by it but also I am better prepared to give an account of my faith to others.

M*editation* is another internal spiritual discipline.

When one thinks of meditation, Christianity is usually not the first thing that comes to mind.

Usually when we think of meditating we imagine someone in a pose with legs crossed and palms facing upward. Yoga doesn't have a copyright on meditation.

In fact, meditation is considered an essential spiritual discipline that provides wonderful opportunities to spend quality time being quiet with the Lord.

- *What is Meditation?*

There are many types of meditation used by various religions, but the actual definition of meditation according to WordNet web is; the continuous and profound contemplation or musing on a subject or series of subjects of a deep or obtuse nature" and "contemplation of spiritual matters."

That being said, no one faith has a monopoly on meditation. Meditation is really quiet contemplation of something. In the Christian's case, meditation is the deep contemplation of something having to do with his or her faith.

Today meditation is used everywhere from yoga to therapy. There are numerous types of meditation that focus on breathing, objects, feelings, and more.

It is designed to help people grow in understanding themselves, the world around them, their faith, and even healing physical and emotional wounds. Christian meditation has its' own history.

Christian meditation is often referred to as *contemplative prayer*. Meditation is found in the Bible in Joshua 1:8 and Psalm 46:10. Mostly monks have used it since the 4th century A.D. Meditation has seen resurgence by Christians in today's world.

- *Why use Meditation?*

If meditation became popular with Hindu and Buddhist practices, should Christians be practicing meditation? The key to practicing appropriate meditation is making sure that it brings you closer to God.

Joshua 1:8, *this book of the law shall not depart out of your mouth, but you shall meditate on it day and night, so that you may observe and do according to all that is written in it: for then you will make your way prosperous, and then you will have good success.*

Psalm 46:10, *Be still, and know that I am God.*

These verses teach us that silence, calm, quiet, stillness and a dozen other synonyms for *meditation* is the key to knowing God.

A relationship with Him is not based on us providing a litany of wants or woes. A relationship is also spending tranquil time with Him in silence and listening to Him talk to us.

Meditation is one of those quiet practices that allow us to clear our minds of what's going on in our world and to relax in the Lord.

It is especially useful when we are feeling disconnected from God or bound up by worries and doubt.

Meditation is a spiritual discipline that allows us to become content in God. It creates a sense of intimacy with Him. It helps us feel present in the Lord.

- *How do we meditate?*

There are two forms meditation that make it simple for Christians to focus on God.

o The first is called *Concentrative Meditation*. In this type the individual focuses on breathing along with one thing, which could be a scripture, image, or sound regarding his/her faith.

By narrowing your focus, the item you want to focus on becomes clearer as you sit silently and just breathe. You learn to let go of everything around you and focus on God.

o Another type of meditation is called *Mindfulness Meditation*. This type of meditation focuses on feelings.

This is a good type of meditation when you want to feel God's presence around you. You allow yourself to sit silently allowing whatever goes through your mind to travel through it, but you don't react to any of the thoughts or images.

• How can we *find time* for meditation?

We live in busy world where finding time alone is not always rewarded. Meditation takes effort and persistence.

We have to be creative and look for opportunities. We may only have a few minutes to be alone with God.

We may find a few minutes before we get out of bed in the morning or during the drive to work. Maybe we can find a peaceful location during lunchtime.

There is a reason that meditation is a spiritual discipline. We have to work hard to be sure we are getting time alone with God.

The internal discipline of **Fasting**.

What is Christian fasting? Specifically, we humbly deny something from the flesh to glorify God, enhance our spirit, and go deeper in our prayer life.

Christian fasting isn't some kind of a work that's commanded by Christ or required by Scripture. However, that doesn't mean that fasting isn't recommended as a part of our spiritual growth.

Acts 13:4 and 14:23 record believers fasting before they made important decisions. Fasting and prayer are often linked together. Luke 2:27 and 5:33 are two good examples.

Fasting is a way to demonstrate to God and to ourselves that we are serious about our relationship with Him. Too often, the focus of fasting is on the denial of food.

However, the purpose of fasting is to take our eyes off the things of this world and instead focus on the Lord.

Fasting in Scripture is almost always a fasting from food. But there are other ways to fast. Anything you can temporarily give up in order to better focus on God can be considered a fast.

Fasting should be limited to a set time, especially when the fasting is from food. Extended periods of time without eating are harmful to the body. Fasting is not intended to punish our flesh, but to focus on God and feed our souls.

Fasting should not be considered a way to diet or lose weight. We do not fast to lose weight, but rather to gain deeper fellowship with God.

Anyone can fast. Some may not be able to fast from food, diabetics for example, but everyone can temporarily give up something in order to focus on God.

Even unplugging the television for a period of time can be an effective fast.   Yes, it's a good idea for believers to fast from time to time.

Fasting is not required in Scripture, but it's highly recommended. The primary biblical reason to fast is to develop a closer walk with God.

By taking our eyes off the things of this world, we can focus better on Christ.

> Matthew 6:16-18 - When *you fast, do not look somber as the hypocrites do, for they disfigure their faces to show men they are fasting. I tell you the truth; they have received their reward in full. But when you fast, put oil on your head and wash your face, so that it will not be obvious to men that you are fasting, but only to your Father, who is unseen; and your Father, who sees what is done in secret, will reward you.*

Now back to our story....

In ancient Greece, Socrates was reputed to hold knowledge in high esteem. One day an acquaintance said to the great philosopher, "do you know what I heard about your friend?"

Hold on a minute, Socrates replied. "Before you tell me anything I'd like you to pass a little test. It's called the Triple Filter Test. Before you talk to me about my friend, it might be a good idea to take a moment and filter what you're going to say."

"That's why I call it the Triple Filter Test. The first filter is TRUTH. Have you made absolutely sure that what you are about to tell me is true?" "No," the man said, "Actually I just heard about it and ..."

"All right," said Socrates. "So you don't really know if it's true or not."

"Now let's try the second filter, the filter of GOODNESS. Is what you are about to tell me about my friend something good?" "No, on the contrary..." "So," Socrates continued, "you want to tell me something bad about him, but you're not certain it's true."

"You may still pass the test. There's one filter left, the filter of USEFULNESS. Is what you want to tell me about my friend going to be useful to me?" "No, not really" the man said. "Well," concluded Socrates, "if what you want to tell me is neither true nor good nor even useful, why tell it to me at all?"

Socrates' internal discipline kicked in automatically because he'd made a decision not to listen to things that may not be best or useful for him in the long run.

Christian mentors should emphasize to mentees the importance of developing the internal disciplines. By practicing the internal disciplines, mentees will be guided by truth to seek after that, which is good, resulting in a better-equipped spiritual toolbox for success in all areas of their lives.

CHAPTER 12

External Spiritual Disciplines

One day a young student was walking with his professor. They saw a pair of old shoes lying beside the path that belonged to a poor man working in a field close by. The man was nearly finished with his day's work.

The student suggested to the professor that they play a trick on the man. "We'll take his shoes and hide behind those bushes, and see how he reacts when he cannot find them."

"My friend," answered the professor, "we should never amuse ourselves at the expense of the poor."

"You are rich and there is a way you may give yourself much greater pleasure through this poor man. Let me suggest that you...."

We'll find out what the professor suggested and what the student learned from this experience at the end of the chapter.

Evangelism is one of the external disciplines

Donald S. Whitney wrote a good article titled: *The Gospel and the Discipline of Evangelism* found on Lifeway.com.

He extols the tenant that the gospel must be clear to believers before they can share it clearly with unbelievers.

It is paramount that mentees have a clear and concise understanding of the gospel and can effectively communicate the gospel to others.

Can a person genuinely understand and believe the gospel and not want to share it with others or seek ways to spread it? The gospel is self-perpetuating.

The Holy Spirit works through the good news to create spiritual life in dead souls. He works through this new life spreading the message of Jesus to others.

New believers love the gospel in a way that compels them to share its message.

The effect of the gospel on the believer's heart is to create an ambassador who wants to evangelize and tell others about the person and work of Jesus Christ. Notice that I said the person wants to evangelize.

For various reasons he may often fail to do so, but the desire is present. The desire isn't based on merely wanting to live up to expectations. Rather, there is a genuine longing to see other people become followers of Jesus.

If these effects haven't occurred in the hearts of those who claim to believe the gospel, at least one of two problems exists.

• They merely have agreed that the gospel is true, thinking that agreement is saving faith and have not actually relied on the gospel for salvation.

• They simply do not understand it.

Evangelism: overflow and discipline

Despite the normalcy of gospel-changed people sharing the good news from the overflow of its effect in their lives, there's still a sense in which evangelism must be a discipline.

It's easy for ambassadors to become so overwhelmed by responsibilities and burdens that they rarely find themselves in situations for meaningful conversations with non-Christians.

Viewing evangelism as a discipline as well as a delight means that we sometimes must make choices. We choose to be with lost people when we'd probably enjoy being with Christians instead. Our hope is to have opportunities to talk with them about Jesus.

We need to remember the gospel is a message we communicate through words about the person and work of Jesus Christ. The *discipline of evangelism* is intentionally conveying those words.

The consistency of our Christian examples may affect the integrity of our witness, but merely watching an example saves no one.

Ultimately it's not actions, important as they are but the words of the gospel that *is the power of God for salvation to everyone who believes,* Romans 1:16.

Jesus' Great Commission for us *to make disciples for Him of all nations* in Matthew 28:19-20 is not incidental or accidental. The intentionality of this supreme task implies and requires discipline.

How might you intentionally create opportunities to speak of the life and work of Jesus?

Service is another external discipline.

God gave us one of the greatest examples of service in the Bible. We call it the Last Supper. Jesus went around the room and washed the feet of His disciples.

Washing another person's feet was a big deal at that time in history. It was a servant's job and a humbling experience.

The disciples looked up to Jesus as a great leader and teacher. Washing of the feet of the disciples was the act of an obedient servant, Jesus Christ.

In this one act Jesus gave an impressive lesson on humility and service. Serving is a privilege and a gift. Service comes in many forms, but in its intent and action we grow closer to God.

John 13:12-16, *12 So after he had washed their feet, and had taken his garments, and was set down again, he said unto them, Know ye what I have done to you? 13 Ye call me Master and Lord: and ye say well; for so I am.14 If I then, your Lord and Master, have washed your feet; ye also ought to wash one another's feet.15 For I have given you an example, that ye should do as I have done to you.16 Verily, verily, I say unto you, The servant is not greater than his lord; neither he that is sent greater than he that sent him.*

- Service is **Faith in Action**

None of us are above serving. It is one of the easiest of the spiritual disciplines put into practice. Youth groups teach this spiritual discipline through outreach ministries, mission trips, and more. Yet going through the motions of service isn't enough.

- Service comes from **the Heart**

Service that is genuine comes from the heart. The true spiritual discipline of service involves putting others' needs before our own.

Intentions are just as important as the actions we perform in service. Sometimes we get so involved in activities that we forget why we are doing them.

Serving can sometimes become a distraction to our faith. It is important that we pray for God to help us keep the right attitudes in serving. That goes hand in hand with prayer for opportunities to do good for others.

Stewardship is another of the external disciplines.

Learning good stewardship over money is an important part of faith and daily life. The Bible mentions money more times than love.

This may seem odd but the love of money can be quite a corrupting emotion. Learning to manage money well can help one be a more responsible Christian and adult.

Jesus relates a parable of The Pounds in Luke 19:11-27 that describes the importance of being good stewards over our faith and our lives. Good stewardship is an important spiritual discipline.

Here are some important ways to demonstrate strong Christian stewardship in your life.

- Understand what you possess *belongs to God*.

Good stewardship means that the things we have, including our money, are blessings from God. All we own belongs to God.

This means that we need to be responsible with the money we earn and how we use it. We should look at our possessions as a treasure God has provided, and understand the privilege of possessing them.

- *Use your treasure wisely*.

If you are blessed with money and things, God trusts you to use those material blessings responsibly. Being a good financial steward does not mean putting your money away and never letting it see the light of day.

It also doesn't mean spending all of it. We use our relationship with God to see how we should use the money and possessions He provides.

- *Give back* to God

It is important that we give back to God in order to properly use the money and things God has given us. We should save money for our children's future college expenses.

We should make sure we give back to God in ways that He instructs and expects. This begins by giving God the tithe.

The tithe is a minimum of ten percent of the income we receive. The tithe is the beginning. Offerings above the tithe should follow.

This means giving what we can to deserving causes inside and outside our local churches. Sometimes good stewardship means going through the things we own and giving them away to those who are in greater need.

- Understand you will *leave all your material goods behind*.

We should put money away for our futures. When our love of things or money comes before our faith we can lose sight of what is important.

Good stewardship is maintaining proper balance between saving and giving. It requires practice and discipline.

We should always keep in mind that no matter how many computers, cars, iPods, shoes, purses, etc. we possess, we will leave it all behind someday. We will stand before God.

We will take with us only those spiritual things that cannot be destroyed by the fires of judgment. First Timothy 6:7, reminds us that good stewards know they can't take the material things they possess with them beyond this earth.

Submission is another Spiritual Discipline

Despite what the world may think, there is nothing weak in being strong in the spiritual discipline of *submission*. However, it is one of the most difficult disciplines to practice.

We want to be independent and strong. But we don't want people to walk all over us. An important part of developing the spiritual discipline of *submission* is to balance being open and humble with knowing when not to let people take advantage of us.

- Submission means *being accountable*.

Christians are accountable to God. We know He sees all that we do and that we should confess our sins to Him.

We are also accountable to others around us. We will be held accountable for our actions. The same can be said with our faith.

We are accountable for our actions in relation to our faith. Outsiders look at our actions and us and develop opinions about God based on what we do. We need to be submissive to God's rule to be good examples to others and to please Him.

Hebrews 13:17, *"Obey your spiritual leaders, and do what they say. Their work is to watch over your souls, and they are accountable to God. Give them reason to do this with joy and not with sorrow. That would certainly not be for your benefit."*

- Submission means being *open to direction*.

We become more open to direction by allowing ourselves to be accountable. Receiving criticism well is difficult.

That is one reason why submission is considered a spiritual discipline. It takes effort to take criticism well. It is easier to be defensive and dismissive of what we're being told is wrong.

When someone has developed the spiritual discipline of *submission* they are able to accept criticism and direction. They not only accept it, they remain open to it.

> Proverbs 28:13-14 - *"People who conceal their sins will not prosper, but if they confess and turn from them, they will receive mercy. Blessed are those who fear to do wrong, but the stubborn are headed for serious trouble."*

- What do we receive by being submissive?

o We learn more about ourselves when we practice the spiritual discipline of submission.

o We become more patient.

o We learn humility.

o We understand how to be honest with others and ourselves.

o We become stronger in our faith because we no longer have to hide our weaknesses from others.

o We are able to listen to others with open minds.

o We break the cycle of thinking of ourselves first.

o We learn to actively place ourselves in God's hands and that allows us to build our relationships with Him.

> *1 Peter 5:6-7 - "So humble yourselves under the mighty power of God, and at the right time he will lift you up in honor. Give all your worries and cares to God, for he cares about you."*

- ## How do we practice submission?

Making the decision to be more submissive is fine, but putting it into action is another matter. There are things we can do to develop this spiritual discipline.

o *Hold your tongue*. Take a moment before you speak to actually listen and absorb what others are telling you.

o *Be discerning*. Don't confuse submission in a spiritual sense with allowing people to take advantage of you. Before you do what others tell you, weigh it against what the Bible teaches.

o *Take yourself less seriously*. We all like to have our ways. Ask yourself if it will really make any difference to try someone else's idea.

o *Examine how you think*. Try looking at why you find yourself having difficulties with being submissive. When do you get angry? Why? When are you most resistant? Ask God to help you see your true self more clearly.

o Take a few hours to be fully submissive to everyone around you while also being discerning and reasonable. Put aside your needs or feelings for a few hours.

Now back to our story...

One day a young student was walking with a professor. They saw a pair of old shoes lying beside the path, which belonged to a poor man working in a field close by. He was nearly finished his day's work.

The student suggested to the professor that they play a trick on the man. "We'll take his shoes and hide them behind those bushes, and see how he reacts when he can't find them."

"My friend," answered the professor, "we should never amuse ourselves at the expense of the poor."

"You are rich and there is a way you may give yourself much greater pleasure through this poor man. Put a coin into each of his shoes, and then we'll hide and watch how the discovery affects him."

The student placed coins in the shoes, and they hid behind some bushes close by. The poor man soon finished his work and came across the field to the path where he had left his coat and shoes.

He slipped his foot into one of his shoes and felt something hard inside the shoe. He pulled the shoe off and found several coins inside.

He looked puzzled with astonishment and wonder at what he held in his hand. He gazed at the coins, turned one over and looked at it again and again. He looked around, but no one was to be seen.

He put the money into his pocket and proceeded to put on the other shoe. But his surprise was doubled on finding coins in the other shoe also.

His feelings overcame him. He fell to his knees, looked up to Heaven and uttered a loud fervent prayer of thanksgiving to God.

He spoke of his sick and helpless wife and his children who had no food. The money from some unknown person would save his family from perishing.

The student was deeply moved and his eyes filled with tears. "Now," said the professor, "aren't you better pleased with what you did rather than what you thought you wanted to do?"

"This has taught me a lesson I will never forget" the student replied. "Now I truly understand the truth of those words, which I never really understood before: It is more blessed to give than to receive."

Truly, it is better to give than to receive. Mastering internal spiritual disciplines will be manifested in outward external actions.

Cultivating external disciplines, outward external actions will generate internal spiritual growth.

Mentors should place strong emphasis on the fact that internal disciplines and external disciplines go hand in hand. Great care and generous time should be spent in helping mentees develop these.

Final Thoughts

The final step for mentors is understanding when to the mentoring process has progressed to the point of cutting the mentee loose. What do I mean by that?

There is a wonderful sense of accomplishment when the mentor sees the mentee's growth and development reach the point of maturity.

How does one know when the mentee reaches this point? That is not an easy question to answer nor is there a standard answer.

I believe that moment comes when the mentee completes assigned tasks, develops spiritual disciplines in his life, shows maturity in his actions and relationships, and is prepared to assume the role of mentor himself.

What about the future? The mentor/mentee relationships can develop into lifelong relationships. Mentors should periodically touch base with mentees.

An occasional phone call or email just to stay in touch is in order. Mentees should also know they have a mentor for life. They have someone they can also touch base with from time to time.

Mentoring Resources

Spiritual Disciplines by Grace Communion International https://www.gci.org/spiritual/discip1

ACCESS online Bible Studies by Randal House Publications

http://www.accessbiblestudies.com

STRESS and TIME MANAGEMENT by Appalachian Bible College

http://www.christiancollegeguide.net/article/subcategory/Stress-And-Time-Management

FAMILY Common Sense by Dr. Roy W. Harris

http://royharris.info/caring-for-the-caregiver/family-common-sense

Common Sense LEADERSHIP by Dr. Roy W. Harris

http://royharris.info/caring-for-the-caregiver/test

The Art of Effective Questioning by Irene Leonard

http://www.coachingforchange.com/pub10.html

Your First Mentoring Meeting by Building Effective Mentoring Partnerships

http://pcaddick.com/page11.html

6 Tips For Mentorees To Prepare For Meetings With A Mentor by Management Mentors

http://www.management-mentors.com/about/corporate-mentoring-matters-blog/bid/88274/6-Tips-For-Mentorees-To-Prepare-For-Meetings-With-A-Mentor

Keeping it Together – Wilson Living Magazine by Dr. Roy W. Harris

http://www.wilsonlivingmagazine.com/magazine/archives/49/786-keeping-it-together

The Jethro Principle - by Archie Luper

http://cconline.faithsite.com/content.asp?CID=28085

<u>Disclaimer</u>: The resources above are only suggestions. The fact that they appear on the list does not mean that Roy Harris' Ministries endorses all the material and information contained in each one.

134

Dr. Harris is in high demand as Conference and Retreat Speaker. He has spoken in 38 American States, Europe, Israel, Kenya, Tanzania, and Uganda ministering in over 400 business organizations, schools, colleges and churches.

Roy began *Roy Harris Ministries* in 2007 as a ministry to help and encourage pastors, churches, Christian educators and Christian businesses.

Roy Harris Ministries' has grown into a multifaceted ministry including but not limited to:

Living Beyond Grief Conferences	Pastor/Staff
Leadership Conferences	Church Renewal
Conferences	Church Evangelism
Conferences	Couples Retreats
Men's Retreats	Family
Enrichment Days	Traditional Church
Revival Meetings	

Go online www.royharris.info for more information on each of these and much more about Roy and how he might help your church, school, or business.

For more information contact Dr. Harris:

roy@royharris.info (615-351-1425)

906 Castle Heights Ave

Lebanon, TN 37087

A book by Roy for those providing care to the terminally ill. For three years Roy provided loving care for his terminally ill wife Diana until her death. He wrote the book to encourage and help those who provide care to terminally ill loved ones and friends and also to help others better understand how to encourage and help caregivers.

What others have said...

"As a caregiver myself (my wife has MS), I was moved, encouraged, helped, comforted, challenged, and blessed. You will be, too." **Robert Morgan,** Senior Pastor, The Donelson Fellowship - Nashville, TN

"This book is a must for every caregiver, pastor, deacon, choir director, youth worker, health care worker, and anyone who wants to better understand how to help and encourage caregivers. Thanks Roy…. Many people will be helped and encouraged by this book." **Stan Toler,** Church of the Nazarene.

Copies of the book may be ordered online at www.royharris.info or www.amazon.com. For an autographed copy send a check for $13.00 (includes shipping) to:

Caring for the Caregiver
906 Castle Heights Ave
Lebanon, TN 37087
For more Information email or call Roy

Roy @royharris.info **615.351.1425**.

LEADERSHIP book by Dr. Harris

Common Sense LEADERSHIP is a unique and practical book every leader will want on his shelf. The book offers a *common sense approach* to *making hard decisions, relationship building, communication, delegating responsibility, receiving and giving criticism, correcting and disciplining others, second guessing past decisions, leadership discernment, conducting business meetings, managing time wisely* and much more.

The book contains an added bonus; a helpful *STUDY GUIDE* conveniently located and the end of each chapter.

Purchase your copy.

Online @ www.royharris.info - Dr. Harris' website. (Also www.Amazon.com)
or send $13.00 for each copy (includes shipping) to:

> **Common Sense LEADERSHIP**
> 906 Castle Heights Ave
> Lebanon, TN 37087
> For more Information email or call Roy
> *Roy @royharris.info* **615.351.1425**.

Help for FAMILIES

FAMILY Common Sense Whether a *Tune up* for your own marriage or a *Tool* encouraging others, you'll find this book a great resource. Dr. Harris lives what he teaches.

Marjorie Workman--*Retired Director of Women Nationally Active for Christ* and *Faculty Member at Welch College* Nashville, Tennessee.

Purchase your copy.

Online - www.royharris.info - Dr. Harris' website. (Also www.Amazon.com) or send $16.00 for each copy (includes shipping) to:

FAMILY Common Sense
906 Castle Heights Ave
Lebanon, TN 37087
For more Information email or call Roy
Roy @royharris.info **615.351.1425**.

Made in the USA
Charleston, SC
05 April 2015